T0283328

LOVING ME
AFTER WE

LOVING ME AFTER WE

The Essential Guide to
Healing, Growing, and Thriving
After a Toxic Relationship

Ginger Dean

FLATIRON
BOOKS
NEW YORK

www.flatironbooks.com

Library of Congress Cataloging-in-Publication Data

Names: Dean, Ginger, author.
Title: Loving me after we : the essential guide to healing, growing, and
    thriving after a toxic relationship / Ginger Dean.
Description: First edition. | New York : Flatiron Books, [2024]
Identifiers: LCCN 2024004880 | ISBN 9781250876669 (hardcover) |
    ISBN 9781250876676 (ebook)
Subjects: LCSH: Separation (Psychology) | Self-esteem. | Interpersonal
    relations. | Man-woman relationships—Psychological aspects.
Classification: LCC BF575.G7 D4364 2024 | DDC 155.6/43—dc23/
    eng/20240205
LC record available at https://lccn.loc.gov/2024004880

Our books may be purchased in bulk for promotional, educational, or business use. Please contact your local bookseller or the Macmillan Corporate and Premium Sales Department at 1-800-221-7945, extension 5442, or by email at MacmillanSpecialMarkets@macmillan.com.

First Edition: 2024

10 9 8 7 6 5 4 3 2 1

To Marin, Maria, and Virginia.

You have been the mirrors that reflected my true self, the healers who tended to my wounds, and the midwives who helped birth the woman I am today.

Thank you for being the sisters and mother figures I always needed but never knew I'd find in you. Your unwavering support, love, and guidance lit up my life in ways you'll never know, and I am forever grateful for the profound impact you've had on my journey of self-discovery.

Contents

LOVING ME
AFTER WE

Introduction

Heartbreak brought you home, back to yourself," my therapist said as I cried through smeared mascara. I'd just gone through the worst breakup of my life.

"Well, this shit hurts!" I sobbed.

"Good," she said. She'd seen me struggle through this relationship, and her honesty was welcome within the bond that we'd built. "Otherwise you'd keep repeating the same patterns with the same jerk, and you wouldn't be here about to embark on the journey back to yourself." She was direct, with a mastery of shifting between the lace glove and iron fist—mirroring my emotional turmoil back to me so I could see how much pain he was putting me through. She'd seen me through the ups and downs, heard me refer to him as a jerk and then forget the next day. She wasn't going to let me get away with anything. I wanted a no-nonsense therapist, and she understood the assignment.

I'd been dating someone who'd make plans, tell me, "I'm on my way," and then not show up. He'd call hours later with an excuse, then apologize and promise to make it up to me. He would bring me gifts and do everything to make sure I'd forget what happened. This pattern left me in tears, wondering why he'd get my hopes up only to not show up physically or emotionally. Still, I was addicted to the constant ups and downs. Part of me wanted him to be sorry and make it up to me. It felt good to hear him apologize. Few people in my life ever had.

Through my therapist's guidance, I came to see that the apologies were never followed up by meaningful change. They were simply a way to manipulate me. She pointed out that it was less about him and more about the pattern that was emerging in my own life and relationships, the toxic roller coaster I couldn't seem to get off of. I relentlessly chased love, affection, and acceptance only to have the door slammed in my face every time. This heartbreak finally forced me to examine the ways that I had been disconnected from myself and my own emotional needs, and how I had focused on finding the love I needed from other people rather than cultivating it within myself.

My therapist showed me the harsh truth I had been afraid to confront: the patterns playing out in this relationship reflected old patterns from my earliest formative relationships. To be fully free and happy, I would need to work to understand the larger picture. At the time, I resisted the idea, but it was clear that she'd seen a version of me in many of her clients over the years. She knew us.

We've all been there—nursing a broken heart, silently wishing things would change, and patiently waiting for the world around us to adjust. It's a hard place to be, isn't it? Sometimes, it feels easier to live with the pain of heartbreak and failed relationships because at least it feels familiar. And you know what? That's okay. It's all part of our journey. At times, we might not be quite ready to look inward and explore our role in these relationships. That's perfectly alright. Embracing our pain and giving it space to breathe is a significant step in our path to healing and growth. (Please note that if you have been in an abusive relationship, your abuser is responsible for that pain, always. However, there are key steps we can take to break the patterns that may repeatedly put us in toxic relationships. These steps are the focus of this book. My goal is that by following them, we can all find happiness and security in love.)

It might be a painful journey, but know that you're not alone. I'm right there with you.

Hitting rock bottom in a toxic relationship often brings us to the painful realization that when a partner fails to love us enough, we also struggle to love ourselves.

When we choose with our wounds, we love from a place of pain. Our deep hunger for connection manifests as desperation. We "love hard" by loving too much, and, in our search for love outside of ourselves, we chase people who cannot or will not love us back.

Even if our efforts aren't reciprocated, we accept the breadcrumbs of affection because they distract us from the truth of who we've become: women who don't feel worthy of love. I understand this all too well because I was once that girl at rock bottom, wondering if there would ever be an end to the cycle of chaos and unpredictable relationships. I wanted someone else to do the hard work of loving me because I didn't feel lovable. But deep down, I knew love shouldn't feel like this. If you're feeling this way too, know that you're not alone. It's hard to be in pain and know that you need to heal when you're not quite sure where to start.

Navigating through the aftermath of a toxic relationship is definitely a roller coaster—it's got its highs and lows, and some days you might feel alone and just plain tired of it all. But hey, I've got your back, and we're going to take this journey together, step by step, until you find yourself again.

My therapist used to tell me that breakups, as tough as they are, bring us back to ourselves, and I've found that to be absolutely true. It's like a doorway to the best version of you, even if it doesn't feel like it right now. I managed to become the strong and loving presence that the younger me really needed, and that's something I believe in for you, too.

This whole experience actually shaped a big part of my career. I'm a therapist, and I've spent a good chunk of my time working with folks who've been through the wringer with difficult and devastating relationships. I've seen it all, and it's become my mission to help people move past the hurt of toxic partnerships and develop into thriving adults.

I started The Inner Circle, an online group membership designed to provide a safe space for women who've been through it all. They come together, heal, share their stories, and find strength in one another. It's not just a support group; it's a community of survivors who are all working toward feeling whole again.

The stories and advice I share with you in these pages are coming from a place of real experience and a genuine desire to help. I've been there, I've helped others through it, and now I'm here to help you. We're in this together, and I believe in your strength to get through this and come out even stronger on the other side.

How might we reframe a traumatic breakup experience as the portal through which we heal and become the best version of ourselves? We have an opportunity to look at trauma and problematic relationships in the context of how they show up in our lives, and discover a new way to work with them instead of simply talking about them.

This won't be a textbook that talks about the "what" of relational trauma. The time has come for us to do more than simply label trauma. We need to understand what it is, why it happens, and what we can ultimately do about it to stop hurting, start healing, and thrive. In this book, we will not only explore romantic relationships, but also consider the context of how the patterns we develop in our early formative relationships are reflected in our adult romantic relationships. In order to do that, we must look at where it all started: what happened, why, and how we can change course today for ourselves and for the generations after us.

This book is divided into three parts. In Part 1, I will talk about the essential steps a person needs to take in the immediate aftermath of heartbreak. Here we will discuss key concepts like hermit mode, the heart sabbatical, Pandora's box, unconscious and conscious commitments, and external healing as opposed to internal healing. Once you are back on your feet, I move on to doing the deep work of internal healing in Part 2. Here we will discuss shadow and ego work, toxic shame, attachment styles, relationship archetypes, individual survival mode and relationship survival mode, and how understanding our internal selves helps us transition into someone who seeks out and sustains healthy relationships. Part 3 is my favorite. This is where we get to dive back into the dating world and use all our hard work. Here I talk about green flags, shared core values, intuition, response versus reactivity, and the new upper limit. Together, the steps, concepts, and exercises in these three parts are key to developing the necessary personal awareness and insights to catalyze monumental change in our romantic relationships. Along the way, I'll share my own experiences and how I used these foundational tools to free myself from a cycle of toxic dating patterns. As someone who has been there, and as a psychotherapist who specializes in helping women break the cycle, I am here to guide you as you start your own healing journey.

You'll learn about the different stages of healing, how to set boundaries, and how to manage difficult emotions. Most important, you'll gain insight into how your formative childhood experiences continue to shape you and your current relationships. In the wake of a breakup, we all vacillate between feeling lonely, anxious, and optimistic, but that's all part of the process. You may even go to therapy for a few months, tackle a few issues, and think you're finished until more pink elephants materialize in your sessions showing you the other areas that need your attention. *Pink elephant* refers to a big, obvious problem that everyone knows about but nobody wants to talk about. It's so obvious and strange, like a pink elephant would be, but everyone's pretending it's not there. It's a way of saying, "Hey, we're all ignoring something really important here." As the journey continues, you'll create healthier boundaries. But realize this also means you need to actually implement and stand by them.

This is what the "deep inner work" means. You'll have days where you're celebrating the brave decisions to walk away from the pain, and others when you want your old life back.

Somewhere along the line, you'll think that if you just journal enough and read enough books, you'll have fully done your part to heal. But eventually you will realize that healing isn't linear; it's an evolutionary process. As you come into this realization, it is also common to be bombarded by negative self-talk and ego-driven stories that try to derail your progress: "You're weak for needing to take time to heal," "If you don't find someone else soon, you'll be alone forever," "You're just wasting time." But I want you to know that these are just stories that your ego creates because healing requires vulnerability and our egos didn't sign up for that.

Unfortunately, we live in a society that encourages women to be soft and submissive for men. Then, when our hearts are broken, we're told to get back out there and find someone new to get over the last one—as if our value as women lies solely in being in a relationship. We have to shake these beliefs off. Our value exists within ourselves, and it's time to reclaim it.

Heartbreak brought me back home to myself, not only in my romantic relationships, but in every other area of my life. As long as I was still hurting and living in survival mode, it was difficult for me to heal and eventually thrive. The lessons were hard, and the journey has been bittersweet, but it has all been worth it.

We can change our narrative. This book is a guide to healing after toxic relationships and a guide to the rebirth of the best version of yourself. I'm here to shine a light on your path toward healing.

Part I

HEALING

1

My Story

My ex-husband and I met in graduate school in our early twenties, got engaged within eight months of dating, and married a year later. We bought our first home with plans to have children once we both were finished with graduate school. Because what else would we do other than continue to check boxes off our list of social expectations for young couples?

We endured the kind of stress that only hustle culture approves of. Our egos simply had to prove that we were good enough to our respective families. We were highly focused on achieving our way out of childhood trauma, and we both had something to prove as first-generation children of immigrants.

Our road to "success" was a roller coaster, but I convinced myself it was worth it to check off those boxes. I can now see that we were trapped in a cycle of emotional addiction that kept me in a never-ending cycle of love-bombing, withdrawal, make-ups, breakups, unpredictable behavior, and physical, emotional, and verbal abuse.

I remember the first time he slapped me in the face. Yes, I was upset and shocked, but we had a trip to see our parents the next day, and I had to pull it together. I turned to MAC

Studio Fix and Naphcon to conceal my black eye. I worried my makeup would melt and reveal the truth of what I was hiding. Embarrassment. Shame. Guilt. I felt I was betraying the woman inside me who was screaming out for help. The woman who knew this wasn't the kind of life or marriage she was meant to have. I still remember constantly checking the mirror to make sure that my concealer was working.

I held on for what would be years. The reality was that I needed help and didn't know how to ask for it. I'd spent so much time being a rock to everyone around me both personally and professionally that I didn't know how to allow someone else to do that for me.

But every story, no matter how bleak, often has a turning point. For me, that moment arrived unexpectedly on a rainy Tuesday evening. I was outside, drenched from the rain and fumbling with my keys. As I stepped into the dimly lit hallway of my home, I heard a phantom sound that stopped me in my tracks. It was the sound of my younger self, from a time before the chaos, laughing without a care in the world.

I slid down the wall, buried my face in my knees, and let out a guttural scream—a blend of pain, frustration, and desperate longing for that lost version of myself. Right then, I realized that I had surrendered my joy, my identity, and my peace to a relationship that didn't value me.

On that day, I made a promise to myself: no more hiding, no more justifying, and no more self-betrayal. It was time for me to reclaim my voice, to take back the reins of my life, and to rediscover the strong, vibrant woman who lay buried beneath years of suppression.

I never spoke up about the abuse I faced from my husband. My family didn't know. My closest friends did not know. Not even my couples' therapist knew. During that period of my life, I felt more shame than I even knew was possible. The shame of being a therapist, and seeing another therapist for help with my marriage. The shame of telling her that the strong and determined woman I cast for her was also being hit and slapped around? I just couldn't do it. I wouldn't share the truth with her. And at the time, I saw nothing wrong with that. That's how deep this was for me. I was going to hide the truth regardless of the sacrifices, regardless of the cost.

Around this time I remember a friend saying to me, "You've changed, and I don't like it. It's like you're this different person. No more light. No laughter. You're not enjoying life. I know it. You know it. But we don't have to talk about it. Just know that I know and when you're ready to talk, I'm here." So, I grinned my way through that exchange while crying inside.

The last time my husband physically assaulted me, I was bloody, bruised, and had a cracked rib. I knew I had to call the police, but it was the hardest thing I've ever had to do. I knew that if I did, my life would change irrevocably. It meant giving up the mask. Still, another part of me knew I couldn't keep living like this. There was no forgiving this. There was no way to unsee this. I was locked out of my home, bloody and bruised for my neighbors to see. There was no way that I could hide what had happened. I didn't want to keep living like this; I deserved better.

I sat outside our door, crying on the phone with the 911 dispatcher. She calmed me down long enough for me to give her my location. The police arrived and took pictures of me exactly where they found me. On the ground, in the corner, hysterical and crying. Part of me was relieved I didn't have to hide the truth anymore, but mostly I was embarrassed.

Pressing charges against him finally gave me the permission to leave.

The officer assigned to my case assured me that my ex had been apprehended a few blocks away and that I was safe. They called my uncle, who came over, and they gave me a safety plan as well as what to expect over the next few days. They arrested my ex, and I was issued a temporary restraining order for seventy-two hours. The officer would later call and visit to make sure I was okay in the days after the incident and leading up to the court date. When I saw him again in court, I gave him a note thanking him for everything he'd done on that day. There are so many different people that help us on our journeys to healing, and he was one of them.

After the divorce, I started seeing a new therapist. I remember asking her, "When will I know that I will be okay after all that I've been through?"

Her answer might be unsettling for some, but it's what I needed to hear at the time, and I deeply feel there is wisdom in confronting this uncomfortable truth: "When you can look at all of this and see the lesson to be learned." She helped me see that, yes, the marriage had to end, for obvious reasons, but the woman who had married that monster had to evolve as well. It took a long time, but I can now call that old version of myself a friend. My lessons were in learning how to let go so that I could grow. Had that day not happened, I cannot say I would have found the strength to leave on my own. I'd talked about leaving, even fantasized about it. But there was no concrete plan in place until that day.

I'd convinced myself that by hiding the truth, I was focusing on the good in the marriage. I didn't understand the emotional somersaults and the resulting wear and tear on my psyche until I was out of it. My health was deteriorating, and I was only in my late twenties. Read that line again. My twenties! But once I filed for divorce, I never looked back.

By leaving him, it made me work harder to break the cycle of emotional addiction, starting my own journey toward healing in all my relationships.

Part of the work I needed to do on my path to healing was to find out why I had stayed in the relationship for so long. In my work as a psychotherapist, I've come to understand it as a pattern of self-abandonment.

Growing up, I was trapped in a tumultuous world of emotional abuse. The constant fighting and physical violence between my parents made me believe that this type of conflict was just a normal thing that happened in relationships. I was drowning in a sea of emotions that I couldn't understand, let alone control. This led me down a path of emotional extremes, and I became addicted to the highs and lows of unhealthy relationships. My marriage would be one that eerily reflected this dynamic.

My struggles with codependency only made things worse.

I found myself drawn to partners who were obsessed with me, and if they weren't, I found them boring. This was my anxious attachment at work, sabotaging my relationships and seeking out intense sexual chemistry that could distract me from my trauma. I was in love with the idea of potential, always looking for someone who could fulfill my needs, instead of realizing that it was up to me to fulfill them. It took a long time, but I finally realized that I needed to love myself more. It was a hard pill to swallow, but once I did, everything else fell into place.

The road to healing was bumpy, but it was necessary for me to take a break from the toxic relationships that were dragging me down. I had to reconnect with myself, to heal my nervous system, and to examine my own attraction to these kinds of relationships, based on my own unresolved emotional wounds. I will discuss all of this in Part 1: Healing.

Above all else, I had to take ownership of my role in the situation and make a decision to change. It wasn't easy, but it was worth it.

I see the process of healing after an abusive, toxic, or simply tumultuous relationship as a journey of self-discovery, one that asks us to dive deep into our unconscious minds and take responsibility for our own healing. It's about becoming more self-aware and empowered to make conscious decisions that align with our values and aspirations.

As you embark on this journey, be prepared to encounter situations and relationships that challenge your newfound sense of self. Your ex may try to creep back in, your family may continue to make inappropriate requests, or new partners may show up with their own issues. You'll start to realize that toxic relationships can show up in all forms, not just romantic, but in this book I will primarily be focusing on how toxic romantic relationships affect us and how you can heal from them. That said, keep in mind that much of what we will be covering also applies to non-romantic relationships.

On this journey, you may even question if you are truly finished with the past, ready to set boundaries or stop playing savior. But at the end of the day, you have to remind yourself that you deserve emotional peace, mutual respect, and emotional safety. You have to own your power and continue to make conscious choices that serve your highest good.

HEALING ISN'T LINEAR

Healing is a journey with twists and turns, meandering through dark valleys and up bright peaks. It's an odyssey that can take you to unexpected places and bring you face-to-face with parts of yourself that you've long kept hidden away. You may experience a flood of emotions and awareness that can feel overwhelming. You may realize that the way you've always understood your life and relationships is no longer true.

It's often painful to unpack your old beliefs and reshape them to fit an updated understanding of the world. Like unearthing an ancient artifact that has been buried deep within the earth for centuries, it's a slow and delicate process, but when you finally uncover it, the beauty is breathtaking. For so long, you've kept your past traumas and unresolved emotions tucked away in your very own Pandora's box. It can be frightening to confront them and let them go, but it's essential to your growth and healing.

These realizations can feel like you're making progress one day, and the next you're right back where you started. You may encounter setbacks and obstacles that make you question if you're making any progress at all. But it's important to remember that healing is a process, not a destination.

Be patient with yourself and embrace the process and all the twists and turns that come with it so that you can appreciate the beauty of the journey as much as the destination. Each step forward, no matter how small, is progress. You're learning to make conscious decisions and intentional commitments so that you can finally heal and thrive.

Buckle up and get ready for the ride of your life. Embrace the journey of healing and self-discovery that brings us back to ourselves. The first stop: unpacking that Pandora's box in the back of your emotional closet.

PANDORA'S BOX

Deep within all of us lies a Pandora's box filled with unaddressed trauma and unresolved emotional wounds that lurk beneath the surface. These forgotten emotions, traumas, and wounds have been pushed aside or ignored in order to survive in past relationships—yet they've covertly influenced our relationships nonetheless. This box holds painful memories surrounding toxic relationships, unhealthy patterns, emotional abuse, abandonment, rejection, betrayal, and more.

Often, we try to push these painful memories aside, pretending they don't exist. Yet they remain, like a heavy anchor weighing you down. The key to freeing yourself from the shackles of these emotional wounds lies in diving into and cleaning out your Pandora's box—like that junk drawer in your kitchen you ignore and keep adding to. To do this, you must journey into the depths of your own psyche, face the demons that have long haunted you, and allow yourself to finally confront them head-on. If you don't, then the same demons in your Pandora's box can show up in your relationships. Your childhood trauma becomes your adult drama.

It's scary and difficult to unearth your past experiences, but the most important element is to remain open to the process. You don't need to be perfect or to remember everything that has made you who you are. It starts with simply declaring that you're listening to your intuition and unconscious mind as they show you the parts of yourself lurking in the shadows of your relationships today. When you do this, your intuition can begin to awaken and denial will soften. Your clarity will sharpen with each layer of trauma you peel back. Like a flicker of light in the darkness, you'll be guided along the path toward healing.

Once you gain the courage to face the demons that haunt you, they can no longer hold you captive to the past. You are now able to trust your intuition, knowing that it will guide you toward the recesses of your heart that hold the answers around how you show up in your relationships. You learn to listen to your inner voice, to heed the red flags that arise, and to make choices that align with your true self.

Start by asking yourself questions such as: *What do I need to know about how my past impacts my relationships today? What are some consistent threads present throughout my childhood and adult relationships? Abandonment? Betrayal? Emotional neglect? Feeling left out?* Try to allow your intuition to guide you to answers.

By normalizing the process of unpacking your old wounds, you can begin to comprehend how they have shaped you and the impact they have on your life today. Embrace the journey, give yourself the grace you deserve, and find solace in the knowledge that we are all in this together.

Only when I opened my Pandora's box was I able to see the patterns that had influenced so many of my relationships. Realizing how my past was still playing a role in them today helped me understand how to break free.

Looking back, a recurring theme emerged in my romantic relationships. I found myself drawn to men who had a pattern of ghosting, breadcrumbing, and unexpectedly severing ties. *Poof*, they were gone—suddenly and without warning. This mirrors the unexpected loss of my father, who passed away without any forewarning. It became evident that I was subconsciously seeking out partners who echoed the abrupt and unforeseen departure of my dad, reinforcing a cycle of sudden and unexplained absences in my life.

Reflecting on my marriage, I realized that something as simple as my ex-husband stepping out to the store would trigger an anxiety deeply rooted in the harrowing moment I learned of my father's passing. From our apartment, I would intently watch him make the short journey across the street to the store and back, my heart heavy with an irrational fear that he might not return. Every departure came with the haunting anticipation of a phone call bearing the worst news. This perpetual state of anxiety was put into stark perspective when a graduate school professor said, "This isn't any way to live; you need to address this," during our group counseling class.

This constant dread of abandonment had become a relentless companion in my daily life, a normalcy I had inadvertently accepted. It was then that I began to deeply reflect on the profound impact of my father's unexpected departure. While my conscious self did not perceive it as an act of abandonment, the vulnerable child within me felt otherwise.

In my friendships with women, I often saw reflections of the complex and unresolved dynamics I experienced with my mother. Echoes of verbal and emotional abuse, abandonment, and the constant fear of rejection manifested in my compulsion to be the ever-accommodating friend, always attending to others at the cost of neglecting myself.

As I matured, I began to recognize that the simmering anger of my twenties was intricately tied to how I was suppressing my genuine feelings. Instead of expressing myself, I was haunted by the belief that voicing my sentiments would lead to rejection.

Professionally, I was fortunate to have an exceptional clinical supervisor. Yet, I couldn't help but project onto her the disappointments I associated with my mother, especially if I lagged in submitting my billing paperwork. When she'd gently ask for a commitment on the completion date, a sense of dread would grip me, and I became convinced that she harbored resentment for my tardiness.

But through her actions, she inadvertently provided a sanctuary for self-reflection. With her warmth, patience, and understanding, she consistently defied my braced expectations of hostility or the cold shoulder.

Eventually I had a stark realization: the shadows I perceived in these relationships were actually my own. It became essential to confront the specters of my past, those that resided in my own Pandora's box. Diving into my Pandora's box, I hit a real "what now?" moment: Do I take the leap and start healing, or just keep everyone else happy while I'm stuck listening to that same old inner voice telling me to play it safe in my relationships?

Unpacking the trauma and unwanted memories you have stored in your Pandora's box is one of the most important steps you will take in your healing journey, and so we will return to this crucial practice at many points throughout the book. It won't be easy, but pushing aside any fear or shame to sort through your Pandora's box is a crucial, and incredibly rewarding, experience.

2

·········

The Decision, Commitment, and Declaration

Stepping into a journey of self-healing often means re-evaluating our relationships. Sometimes, this introspection can lead to the daunting realization that for genuine growth, certain ties might need to be severed or reshaped.

Changing or ending relationships is never easy, and it can be especially difficult when you have invested time and energy hoping for a different outcome. When you've shared emotional experiences with another person, it is natural to feel a sense of loss and to grieve the future you had planned together.

However, it is important to remember that self-love often means choosing between staying in a relationship that no longer meets your emotional needs and making the brave decision to walk away. This is one way heartbreak brings you back home to yourself. You may have spent a lifetime self-abandoning and ignoring your core emotional needs. Now, it's time for you to learn how to rebuild the relationship you have with yourself after neglecting it in favor of chasing relationships with others. By getting in touch with our emotional needs, we get a clearer picture of who we are, what we're looking for, and how we want to feel in our relationships.

I cared for my ex deeply, but there came a point when I realized that I was constantly pushing my own feelings aside for his sake. It was like I was replaying the same old tapes from my childhood.

Now, I've learned how to refocus on my own emotional needs. For example, I prioritize self-validation, knowing I don't need anyone else to tell me I'm enough, and I certainly don't need to perform or audition to "be enough" either. I've laid down clear boundaries, which means I've defined the lines of what's acceptable and what isn't for me in relationships. I've become more in tune with my feelings, thanks to being more self-aware. I work hard to ensure that all my relationships have a balanced give and take.

There's also the importance of tuning into my emotions and truly listening to what they're telling me. That's why I prioritize self-care now. It's all about acknowledging, respecting, and addressing my feelings, ensuring that I'm mentally and emotionally balanced. I make it a point to stay authentic and be true to what I feel. And when things get tough, drawing on my resilience instead of folding like a lawn chair reminds me that every challenge is a chance to grow.

I've learned the importance of emotional growth, staying open, and adapting, and I make sure all my interactions are rooted in respect and accountability. By keeping these emotional needs in mind, I'm making sure I never push my own feelings to the side again.

This powerful yet daunting act of self-love is the most loving and compassionate thing I could have done for myself. Here I was, making the profound shift to honoring my own emotional needs in ways I never thought I had permission to do.

But getting here was no easy feat. I had made an unconscious commitment to sticking out the relationship because I was fearful of starting over and never finding someone else. This type of belief is rooted in ego. It says that in order for me to be valuable to the world, I have to be in romantic proximity to a man. When I say "ego," I'm talking about that inner voice that's been shaped by what society or others think of us. It's that pesky little whisper that sometimes makes us believe our worth comes from outside validation, like staying in a relationship regardless of whether we are happy and safe. So when I say my belief was "rooted in ego," I mean it was more about wanting to fit into societal expectations than truly listening to what my heart and soul were telling me.

Staying meant battling an internal emotional storm that I could no longer withstand, which resulted in many failed starts around ending the relationship. He was sinking deeper into his own emotional quicksand, and he wanted me to save and take care of him, but doing that meant losing myself in the process. It meant becoming his caregiver, acting as his therapist even when I wasn't working professionally as one. It meant losing myself to save him, and that wasn't an option.

Healing requires a decision, a declaration, and a commitment. The decision to heal means declaring this new truth to your support system (friends, family, psychotherapist, treatment team, etc.) and committing to the journey, no matter how turbulent and nonlinear it might be.

THE DECISION

Making the decision to leave wasn't easy. I struggled with feelings of guilt, sadness, and confusion. But in the end, I knew that it was the right decision for me. It was tempting for me to point fingers at him for the issues in our relationship. However, I had to take a hard look in the mirror and acknowledge the times I might have abandoned or betrayed my own needs and feelings for the sake of our relationship.

You may be at the same crossroads or wrestling with a similar decision, and I want you to know that you can never go wrong in choosing yourself in order to heal. As you approach that decision, you might experience a string of events that give you insight into what has been holding you back. To fight through this, you need to acknowledge and shed your unconscious commitments.

UNCONSCIOUS COMMITMENTS

Unconscious commitments are the promises and agreements you make with yourself without ever being aware of having made them. These commitments can take many forms, such as a belief that you are not worthy of love and won't find anyone else if you do leave a toxic relationship, or a feeling that you need to sacrifice yourself for the happiness of others. They can also manifest as feelings of guilt, shame, or fear that prevent you from making the decision to leave a toxic relationship.

As you embark on this journey to healing, you must first recognize the insidious nature of your unconscious commitments. These hidden promises and agreements that you've made with yourself can keep you chained to toxic patterns that prevent you from making meaningful changes. Like roots that anchor you to old patterns, they can be hard to recognize and even harder to change. Unconscious commitments are often deeply ingrained in your psyche, and breaking free from them requires a great deal of self-awareness, courage, and compassion. It's not always a simple decision to walk away, especially when you're confronted with past traumas that have shaped beliefs about yourself and the world around you.

But when you finally do recognize these unconscious commitments for what they are, the grip they hold on you will start to loosen. You can begin to question the beliefs that have been holding you back, and you can start to make conscious decisions that align with what you really need to feel safe and happy in your relationships.

Again, I have to remind you: this journey is not an easy one. Be patient with yourself as you heal. With each step you take toward breaking free from your unconscious commitments, rebuild the commitment to yourself to heal.

THE (CONSCIOUS) COMMITMENT

Ah, the commitment. When the healing gets tough, that's usually when your resistance shows up, especially when things aren't going as you imagined. You'll even question the need for change as the journey forces you to make hard decisions that might result in a dry phone and fewer social outings. But re-member, healing isn't a linear journey, and growth doesn't come from staying in your comfort zone.

It's tempting to wait for someone else to change before you commit to your own growth. Maybe your ex comes back, or the person who ghosted you wants another chance. But we both know where that road leads—down the path of restarting painful cycles all over again.

When you commit to yourself, everything changes. Like a key unlocking a door, you'll start to understand the patterns that have held you back for so long. You'll gain new insights and awareness, and the connections to your past will become clearer. With each step, you'll be climbing higher toward an unshakable self-love. This journey takes time, and it's import-ant to be kind to yourself along the way.

For me, the decision to leave wasn't just about packing my bags and moving out. It was a powerful commitment to prior-itize my own happiness above anything else, even if it meant walking away from the future I had planned.

It wasn't an easy decision. The pain was palpable, and the thought of leaving everything behind was terrifying. But in that moment, I realized that staying in the same place that hurt me would only delay my healing journey.

Looking back, I can see that the decision to leave was just the first step in taking responsibility for my own happiness. Al-though I questioned my decision at the time, it taught me the importance of self-love and the power of making commitments to myself. I learned that sometimes, we need to put ourselves first and prioritize our own well-being above everything else.

So, take a deep breath and commit to the journey of healing and growth. The resistance may be strong, but you are stronger. And when your strength gets tested, you'll also be learning how to allow your support system to show up for you. This is why declaring your intention to heal is important. It allows you to signal to those around you that you're on a new journey to heal.

THE DECLARATION

You've made the bold decision to embark on a journey of self-discovery and healing. You've recognized that the patterns of the past no longer serve you and it's time to take charge of your life. But this isn't a solo journey—you need support.

It's time to make a declaration to those around you that you are committed to your healing journey. This declaration isn't just about words; it's about actions. It's about turning down dates with the same old toxic types and being selective about who you spend your time with. It's about consciously choosing to stop entertaining relationships and situations that drain your energy.

Healing isn't linear and it certainly isn't all love and light. Instead, there are contradictions, false starts, and many shades of gray in between, especially when you've decided that you want to stop repeating painful patterns. Roadblocks will appear, whether it's your ex popping up when you've said you're done, an annoying family member wanting to "borrow" money when you're setting boundaries, or a new romantic potential wanting a parent rather than a partner. All of this is normal and to be expected. Some issues might involve digging deeper—maybe it seems like you're "booked and busy," but really you're dealing with high-functioning depression. We have to start with an awareness that things need to change and that we can't revisit the same places. Think of this as your unconscious mind bringing up things for your review. Why? Its goal is to make you whole.

You're shifting out of autopilot, survival-mode relationships where you made unconscious decisions and moving toward conscious commitments for a healthy and thriving life.

YOU HAVE TO CHOOSE TO HEAL, AGAIN AND AGAIN

I want to share a story about my client Elena that vividly showcases the process of making a decision, standing firm in that declaration, and wholeheartedly committing to the healing journey. You'll be able to glimpse into how these steps play out in real-life scenarios. Let's dive in.

Elena, with her fiery red hair and bubbly energy, was the magnet in any room. People just gravitated toward her. But her love life? It was like a rerun of *Sex and the City*. Sometimes, she wondered if the universe was playing a prank on her, pairing her with guys who never wanted the same thing, or only pretended to, and things would eventually fizzle out.

Her phone was always lit with notifications, thanks to the dating apps. Big words and sweet promises, but mostly just guys looking for attention in the moment. Every now and then, she'd think, "Okay, is he the plot twist?" But it was the same old script.

Then, Jeremy happened. He was good-looking, charming, and seemed genuinely interested. But as days rolled into weeks, Elena felt like she was just a scene in his Netflix rom-com. The real blow came when she spotted his online world, full of escapades that made no room for her.

Heartbroken and confused, she vented in our sessions. And here's where I dropped a metaphorical bomb. "Elena, would you run a marathon on a broken leg?" She blinked, not following. I continued, "Can you heal a broken heart if you keep letting the same kind of people break it over and over again? How do you make space for someone healthy to come in if you're always entangled with the same toxic types?"

That hit hard. It was Elena's "Aha!" moment.

Later at home, in the quiet of her room, tea steaming by her side, she made the big decision. First, those dating apps? Adios. Those messages filled with empty flattery? Trash bin. And Jeremy? Along with memories of past relationships? Blocked. Blessed. Deleted.

With no distractions, Elena started facing her old wounds. She began unpacking memories, understanding her patterns, and re-evaluating her choices. The realization had hit her: she needed to heal. Sure, it wasn't all sunshine. There were nights she'd question her choices. But she'd remind herself of the marathon metaphor and stay committed to her healing journey.

One evening, with her friends sprawled around her cozy

living room, Elena took a deep breath. She knew this would be a different kind of conversation, but it was time.

"Hey, so, I've got something to say," she began, capturing their attention. "You all know how much I value your support and love. And I know you all have the best intentions for me. But I've decided to take some serious 'me' time."

She paused, looking at each face, wanting them to truly understand. "So, here's the thing: No more setting me up on dates, okay? Even if he's a ten out of ten and loves dogs. And, when I call you bored on a Saturday night, remind me not to dive back into old situationships, okay? No matter how appealing it seems in that moment.

"You might see me tempted to call up that situation for a Netflix and chill night, and I need you to tell me to chill. There might be nights when I'm itching to just dress up and head to our favorite spots, hunting for someone new. But what I'll really need then is just a shoulder, maybe a movie night, or just dancing in our pajamas in the living room. I'm in my healing era, giving attention to the old wounds rather than covering them up with messy distractions."

Nods and murmurs of understanding spread around the room. One friend piped up, "So, more popcorn nights and fewer bar nights?"

Elena chuckled. "Yeah, something like that. I'm on a self-love journey. So, bear with me, okay?"

She was met with a chorus of affirmations and hugs. They got it. And Elena felt lighter knowing her tribe was with her on this.

Emerging from her heart sabbatical, Elena had a newfound glow about her—a testament to the profound truths she'd unearthed. Unpacking her Pandora's box brought forward patterns eerily familiar from her younger days, scenes she wished were long-forgotten but had, in fact, become the haunting background score of her life.

Growing up, Elena was the silent observer to her mother's love saga. Memories of her mother—eyes fixed on the silent phone, hoping for a call that rarely came—were etched into Elena's mind. The muffled sobs her mother believed she hid so well had been Elena's lullabies, while those whispered chats with friends about demeaning comments and emotional cold wars served as cautionary tales Elena had promised herself she'd never live.

When Jeremy had entered the scene, past and present blurred, stirring up feelings of uneasy familiarity. Jeremy's unpredictable messages had kept her in a perpetual state of anxious anticipation. The "lighthearted" jabs he'd throw at her dreams during gatherings, only to brush them away later, reminded her so much of the men who once belittled her mother. Arguments with Jeremy were punctuated by days of radio silence, echoing the neglectful men from her mother's tales. In response, Elena had often found herself going above and beyond, preparing his favorite meals or showering him with surprises, all to catch a fleeting moment of the warmth she once had with him.

Yet, just like her mom, Elena wore a mask of happiness. She shrugged off Jeremy's "playful" digs and reassured worried friends with a smile. But in solitude, every sly comment and indifferent gesture ate at her confidence. Lying in her bed at night, Elena's thoughts raced—was she too demanding? Was this the norm for love? The parallels between her love life and her mother's were impossible to ignore.

Acknowledging this painful mirroring was a jolt for Elena. She realized she was caught in a loop, reenacting her mother's heartaches. But with this epiphany came empowerment. Elena knew she had to break the cycle, to write a love story where she wasn't an afterthought but the shining lead. It was her right, her time, and she was poised to embrace it.

And guess what? She wasn't the only one. Many of my clients, and women far and wide, have taken this time-out, dug deep, and emerged more resilient by forging a stronger relationship with themselves.

This is your chance to reclaim your power and live a life that aligns with your values. It's time to break free from the unconscious wounds of childhood and step into a life of conscious loving of yourself and others. But in order to do so, you must declare your intentions to someone you trust, someone who will keep you accountable when the going gets tough. Remember, this is your journey, and you have the power to create the life you deserve. Make your declaration, take action, and watch as the universe conspires to help you heal and thrive.

When I finally declared to my own therapist that I was ready to give up this path of destruction once and for all, she helped me articulate and understand how my inner child had been running my emotional show up until this point. Her guidance and mentorship during our time together was invaluable as I gained deeper insights into my own patterns— insights I would not have garnered had I not declared my intentions to her.

Drawing inspiration from my therapeutic journey, we sought to replicate this atmosphere of discovery and accountability in our Inner Circle membership. There, women find the encouragement to choose their own paths to healing, declaring their intentions within a sisterhood that holds them tight. Mirroring the guidance I received from my therapist, they too embrace insights into their intricate patterns.

Much like them, I unearthed facets of myself I'd long ignored. I discovered that my inner child loved moonlighting as Bob the Builder: a people-pleaser whose value was caught up in working for love. I made my ex the new project, cracked my knuckles, and got to work. This conveniently allowed me to ignore the parts of myself that needed my attention, like the unconscious commitment to thinking I needed to work to earn love by building him into the man I wanted him to be. I became his therapist, mama, cook, and chauffeur, which left no room for romantic or passionate love. I was the workhorse in the relationship.

My own heart was neither a haven nor a hospital for myself, but it was for others. In therapy, I learned that this pattern became entrenched during my childhood. Growing up, my mother saw me as an extension of herself, not as an individual with her own needs. Consequentially, I saw my worth grounded in what I did for other people and/or whether they saw me as valuable to their lives. Whether it was wanting to be the thinnest or helping my partner build his businesses, I tried whatever I could out of a deep desire to be loved. But I was tired. And then one day, I hit rock bottom.

I didn't like who I'd become—a shell of a person. I had

no sense of self outside of the relationships I had with others. Through messy mascara and soiled tears, I knew the only place to go was up. I didn't know where I was headed, but continuing to marinate in a pool of my own tears was no longer an option.

Diving deep into my own story, I uncovered this dance I'd been doing for ages. It's like being caught in a seesaw of wanting to pull people super close because of my anxious attachment, then almost shape-shifting into whatever I thought they wanted to keep the peace. It's that fawning response, you know? I was people-pleasing to avoid conflict, and to avoid my own emotions. It felt like I was constantly trying to dance around emotional landmines. Here's what helped me:

Mindfulness Meditation: This wasn't about sitting in a quiet room with candles. Meditation allowed me to clearly identify moments where my anxious attachment was pushing me to cling, or when my fawn response triggered self-abandonment. By grounding myself in the present, I learned to recognize and resist these urges.

Establishing Boundaries: I always thought boundaries would make me come across as "too much." But you know what? An anxious heart often believes that boundaries push people away. In reality, boundaries are expressions of self-respect. I began to understand that it's not only okay but necessary to communicate my needs, without fear of driving someone away.

Seeking Therapy: My therapist? Game-changer. We dug into some old stories, and man, it made things clearer.

Seeing where my fears came from was like turning the lights on in a dim room. With my therapist's guidance, I unraveled how past experiences were the culprits behind my attachment fears and my tendency to appease. By understanding the root, I could address the symptom.

Journaling: Writing gave me a mirror to my subconscious. As patterns emerged on paper, I could pinpoint triggers and situations where my fawning or clinging tendencies took over. For example, if something triggered that clingy or people-pleasing side, I'd jot it down.

Self-soothing Techniques: It sounds cliché, but when the emotional roller coaster hit, just taking a moment, feeling my feet on the ground, and breathing deep . . . it made a world of difference. Over time, deep-breathing exercises and grounding techniques became my go-to during intense emotional tides, giving me a moment of pause to decide how I genuinely wanted to act.

Once I was armed with these tools, and using them consistently, the transformation began. Things started shifting. The once-overwhelming urge to cling began to diminish. The habitual need to pacify or change myself to avoid conflict started to wane. Instead of being tossed around by emotional tempests, I found myself navigating with intention. I could actively choose my responses rather than being instinctively yanked by old patterns.

So, if you're feeling like you're in a maze right now, trust me: it's not forever. It's a chapter, and there's a whole lot of book left. It's perfectly okay if you're in the midst of this emotional whirlwind. Recognize it as a chapter, not the entire story. The pain, the confusion—it's all forging a path to a brighter, freer you. Each challenge is a stepping stone, leading to a stronger, genuine, and beautifully empowered version of yourself. Hold on; the journey is worth every teardrop and every revelation.

3

·· · · · · · · · ·

Hermit Mode

Haley walked into my office with a broken heart, her eyes red and swollen from crying all night. She collapsed into the chair across from me, barely holding back tears.

"I just don't know how to let go," she said, her voice almost a whisper.

"What makes it hard for you to let go?" I asked softly.

She shook her head. "I don't know. I mean, the relationship was so toxic. Everyone around us knew it wasn't healthy. But I can't help feeling like I'm betraying myself by ending it."

I nodded. "I can understand wanting peace but not being quite ready to let go of the chaos."

She looked up at me, tears streaming down her face. "Exactly. I just feel so lost."

We talked about her past relationships and how they all had a similar pattern of fighting and breaking up, only to make up and start the cycle all over again.

"I know this must be exhausting," I said.

Haley nodded, still in tears. "And I just don't know how to stop. I don't know how to set healthy boundaries."

As we unpacked her Pandora's box in our therapy sessions, I learned that Haley had grown up in a dysfunctional family with distant parents who never modeled healthy relational dynamics. We talked about her past traumas, including a toxic work environment that mirrored her childhood home, with parents so preoccupied with their own toxic dynamics they had ignored Haley's emotional needs around connection and validation. It became clear that Haley had a pattern of betraying her emotional needs so that she wouldn't feel lonely, even if it meant staying in abusive relationships.

"It's all you've known," I said. "But it doesn't have to be all you know."

Haley wiped away her tears and nodded. "I know. I just don't know where to start."

We often embark on our healing journey after a tragic event brings us to our knees. In those dark moments, we contemplate our life and the changes that need to happen for us to live better. Otherwise, we reinforce that it is more important to be in codependent, even toxic love than it is to love ourselves enough to break away from:

- Broken hearts
- Distant relationships
- People-pleasing
- Boundary violations
- Living and marinating in a perpetual trauma response
- Immature parents
- Dysfunctional family dynamics
- Toxic work dynamics

- Stressful co-parenting situations
- Betraying our emotional needs to avoid feeling lonely
- Staying in abusive relationships because it's all we know

Take a deep breath and feel the resolve building. You know this can't be all there is to life and relationships. There has to be a different path. You might be here if you've hit rock bottom or found yourself at a dead end in the relationship you have with others or yourself. The pain and despair can take your breath away when you consider the impact and consequences of your decisions and how they've shaped the path that brought you to this exact moment. It's at this place that you might find yourself entering hermit mode.

Maybe you've crash-landed here after a breakup. You hate everyone who wants to get close to you, but you're also struggling with loneliness and rigid boundaries. Sometimes, all you want is to shut the world out, even when that loneliness is hitting hard. It's a tricky spot: wanting to keep everyone at arm's length, but also wanting, well . . . someone. And it's super tempting to make snap decisions just to fill that void. That's where those consequential decisions come into play. Like, maybe pulling someone new into your life on a whim, and before you know it, you're all tangled up. Is it genuine connection, or just a knee-jerk reaction to not wanting to feel alone?

Deep breath. Let's try to sit with those feelings, not run from them. Rushing won't mend your heart faster. Remember, reacting on a whim might lead to detours, more pit stops, and rebound tours. Taking it slow and feeling through it all will pave the way for healthier, conscious love.

The primary relationship you have is with yourself, and during this stage, it's the one that matters the most. You can heal while being in a healthy relationship, but only if you're also in a healthy relationship with yourself. You have to make sure you aren't choosing unhealthy relationships due to your vulnerable emotional state and unchecked destructive patterns. Make sure you have healthy boundaries, good standards, solid core values, and deal breakers you're willing to stand by. Without this key step, you risk returning to old patterns, choosing toxic and tumultuous people, or even jumping into another trauma bond.

When you are in a raw state, your feelings are valid, but they may not be your best guides for finding new, meaningful, and healthy love. Often, after a breakup, you feel unlovable, so you seek attention more than anything else, even if it means tolerating hurtful behavior. It's completely natural to need this validation when you are heartbroken. However, at this stage in your healing, when you seek love in a new partner instead of through friends, self-care, and other sources, you can end up with a partner who reflects your current emotional state back to you in their behavior. Instead of attention from a dating app, what you really need is someone like a friend or therapist to tell you that you matter. It's perfectly fine to tell your friends that you need them to love you a little extra during this time. At this stage, it's also best to indulge in copious self-care and consistent self-soothing while surrendering to the feelings that come up.

I remember when Haley sat on the couch in my office, fidgeting with her fingers as she tried to explain her decision to take time away from dating after her recent breakup. It was a decision that had surprised both of us, as Haley had always been the type to jump back into the dating scene as soon as possible.

"What's changed this time?" I asked her gently, trying to understand her thought process.

Haley sighed deeply, her eyes filling with tears. "I just feel so uncertain of my place in the world," she admitted. "I'm questioning who I am now that I'm open to . . . healing. I crave connection, but I also feel so disconnected from myself that I don't want to be social. It's this constant internal battle."

I nodded, listening closely as she continued to share her thoughts. "I question whether I'm making the right decision to distance myself from certain relationships," she said. "But at the same time, I'm starting to love not having so much relationship drama! It's hard to feel so lonely, but I'm starting to meet excommunicated parts of myself, which oddly enough makes me feel less lonely."

There was a moment of silence as Haley took a deep breath. "I'm feeling conflicted about choosing myself after a life of trying to get others to choose me so that I wouldn't have to," she said softly. "It's hard, but I know it's necessary."

I nodded in a show of support. "It's okay to feel uncertain and conflicted," I told her. "But it's important to honor your feelings and trust your instincts. Taking time for yourself is a brave and necessary step toward healing and growth."

Haley nodded, wiping away her tears. "Thank you, because this is hard," she said quietly.

I smiled at her, feeling grateful that she trusted me enough to share her innermost feelings and conflicts. "Of course," I said. "That's what I'm here for."

Haley's thoughts had bubbled up because she was entering into hermit mode. Before, she had been stuck in a cycle of unhealthy yet familiar relationship dynamics, jumping right back in where she left off, going from breakup to make-up to breakup. For once, she let herself breathe. Now, she was experiencing conflicting feelings that made her question that pattern she had been stuck in before. She'd begun to peel back the onion, and while it was painful, with each layer she was gaining more guidance around what she needed to properly heal.

A mental shift often happens at this time. Instead of porous boundaries and emotional neediness, during hermit mode, it's not uncommon to experience:

A NEED FOR RIGID BOUNDARIES

You hate everyone. You can't fathom going on another date, attending another family function, going out with your friends, or being in a social mood. You hate being alone but prefer it if it means not jumping back into the same situation you just prayed to get out of. Or that you're still dealing with. You build walls around yourself to maintain the taste of inner peace you've gotten.

A CYCLE OF EMOTIONAL
TURBULENCE AND WITHDRAWAL

Your heart is raw, and with that comes good and bad days. On good days, you're twirling around your home like Thumbelina. On bad days, you're struggling to make sense of everything that's happened, and all the feelings you've been avoiding come rushing back. This is the difference between hyperarousal, a state often characterized by anxiety, panic, and feeling out of control, and hypoarousal, where you might feel immobilized, unable to leave your bed or take care of basic hygiene needs. Your brain is trying to adjust to the new normal, without the "happy chemicals" this person/situation once provided. (More on that later.)

It's essential to be intentional about having self-compassion for this process and recognizing that there's nothing wrong with you. Your primary goal and task here is to practice regular self-soothing and self-care because it is the time you're most prone to starting a rebound tour. The loneliness you feel during this time is so excruciating that you might be willing to risk your healing for momentary pleasure with someone you know isn't good for you.

Deep down, you know you're not ready for a new relation-ship, but you choose them because you know it won't last long. This is when attachment wounds enter the room, and it's crucial to remember that we're not doing this anymore.

If you choose to accept the rebound tour mission, you must not break the cardinal rule: don't get attached. If you do, you'll remain stuck at that pit stop while trying to get over your ex.

The pit stop is a placeholder; you may not even really "like" them, but because you haven't yet healed, you are in danger of feeling way too attached to let go and walk away. Not only are you trying to get over your last relationship, but now you've added this relationship to the pyre of dead relationships, intensifying the pain and prolonging the healing process.

A DEEP YET PROFOUND LONELINESS

Loneliness is often seen as negative, but it doesn't have to be! When healing after a toxic relationship, take this opportunity to pause for emotional growth and self-exploration. No one prepares us for these moments, but they offer a unique chance to get closer with ourselves. There is so much power in embracing them.

This loneliness happens because you've finally given yourself space to process. You've stepped out of the cycle, and now your brain has gotten a taste of what it's like to not be so emotionally dependent on another human for your self-worth, happiness, and well-being. You might not be sure you ever want to date again because right now, the prospect of allowing someone in feels overwhelming and scary. This is normal, and there's nothing wrong with being here. This is your mind, heart, and body working in concert to recalibrate your nervous system—you can't heal in the environment that hurt you. You need to take a step back, refocus, and recalibrate.

CONFLICTING FEELINGS
AROUND NEWFOUND SOLITUDE

No one prepares you for the range of conflicting emotions when you're no longer connected to unsafe relationships. You start to realize how much they contributed to you "feeling alive," because at least you were with someone instead of being alone, but you also realize how much of a huge source of stress and drama they were. On one hand you liked the attention, even if it was negative attention. On the other hand, was the negative attention worth the stress, sleepless nights filled with uncertainty, and bad behavior? The path toward emotional growth can be a rocky one, filled with confronting uncertainty and doubts about the players in your relationships as well as your role in them.

You might find yourself needing to shed old versions of yourself, questioning who you truly are and who you want to be. While this process can be liberating, it can also leave you feeling lost and unsure of your identity.

Craving connection is a natural human instinct, but when you're healing, it can feel like an impossible task. You might feel disconnected from yourself, struggling to find the motivation to be social or interact with others. The desire for companionship can be intense, yet at the same time the thought of opening up to someone else can be terrifying.

As you distance yourself from unsafe relationships, you might start questioning whether you're making the right decision. The fear of loneliness can make you doubt your choice to let go of toxic people and situations. You might feel guilty for prioritizing your well-being and wonder if you're being too selfish. You might even be called "selfish," but this is okay. Your path isn't about other people, particularly those who are committed to misunderstanding you. And they're allowed to have and own their conflicting feelings about your healing journey—as it makes them question their own path. It's okay to be understanding of their own inner conflict while honoring the new boundaries that will allow you to move forward.

As you delve deeper into your healing journey, you may encounter painful emotions that you've been avoiding. These feelings can be intense and overwhelming, but they offer an opportunity to meet parts of yourself that you've excommunicated. By confronting these emotions, you may begin to feel less lonely and more connected to yourself.

Choosing yourself goes against a lifetime of trying to get others to choose you instead. You may feel guilty for putting yourself first, and conflicted about whether you're making the right decision. But remember, choosing yourself is the first step toward building a healthier, happier life.

This is your sign that it's time for self-care.

EMBRACING LONELINESS

Remember that there's nothing wrong with taking time away from dating while exploring the difficult feelings that come up post-breakup. I recommend three key steps to my clients for navigating loneliness during this time. Once you've taken

LOVING ME AFTER WE

these steps toward rebuilding your sense of self, you'll be ready whenever love comes knocking once again.

Step One: Acceptance and Presence

Self-forgiveness is key to releasing the past and making the journey to personal development and emotional exploration easier. It's important to own your feelings and not personalize the behaviors of others who lack accountability due to their own wounds. Accountability makes sure you focus on the impact over the intention.

When you accept the present moment without judgment or criticism, you become more present with yourself and your emotions. Embracing loneliness for what it is opens this door to living in the moment and growing from it. Taking the time to check in with your emotions each day can help you identify why you are feeling disconnected or lonely so that you can address those feelings in healthy ways. This could mean taking a walk outside in nature, journaling about your thoughts and feelings, or engaging in any activity that brings you joy.

Step Two: Creating Space for Reflection

Dating can be a growth experience that allows you to see yourself through the eyes of another. As we journey through life, each person we date leaves a mark on our hearts and souls. They're not just stepping stones or chapters in our story; they're co-authors, even if just for a brief time. When we reflect on past relationships, it's like peering into a mirror, revealing our triggers, hopes, and growth areas.

Toxic partners can be a mirror for the unhealed parts of yourself that make you vulnerable to abuse. Remember, triggers are doors to the parts of our souls that need to be addressed to make us whole again. Try not to see these relationships as failures but rather as lessons that teach you the answers to relationship tests, so you can stop repeating the same patterns in your relationships.

It's less about "using" these experiences, and more about cherishing the lessons, understanding our patterns, and embracing the journey toward the kind of love we truly seek. Every relationship, no matter how fleeting or deep, adds a unique shade to our canvas of love and life. Recognizing and interpreting these patterns can be the catalyst for making positive changes and better understanding yourself within the context of your relationships. The issues from our past keep repeating themselves until we interrupt the pattern, understand the origin, and stop the cycle of abuse.

In order to recognize these patterns, we need to make time for quiet reflection. Once you're able to sit with your emotions, you can broaden this experience and create space for reflection without self-judgment. You need time to reflect on what happened in order to gain an understanding of your own experiences and behaviors so you don't re-create similar patterns down the line. Taking this time to reflect can also help you uncover areas where you need more self-love and acceptance so that you look within rather than outwardly seeking validation through relationships with others.

During this period of reflection, try not to place expectations on how quickly you should "move on" or judge your feelings. Remember, some days just suck, and that's okay. One messy day or week won't derail your healing journey because, as we've talked about, healing isn't linear. And there is no "end" to the journey, because we're always evolving. It takes however long it takes, but I promise something better lies ahead if you can sit with and reflect on the good and bad days.

Step Three: Learning to Value Your Own Company

Valuing your own company is key when navigating loneliness. Try doing activities alone such as taking yourself on a date by going out for dinner or seeing a movie solo. These little acts of bravery can help build confidence while allowing you to focus on personal growth instead of relying on external validation. Allow yourself to do something new each day free from shame; learning new skills builds self-esteem while also helping you stay connected with your purpose in life.

If you're feeling overwhelmed by the prospect of dating again after being in a toxic relationship, remember that there is nothing wrong with setting boundaries for yourself first before diving back into the dating world. Taking time for self-care is essential. Give yourself grace as you take steps toward healing—it takes time to get your mind and heart ready to love yourself and others again.

While speaking with my client Haley, I did my best to validate the loneliness she was feeling by normalizing it as a part of the process. I helped her navigate the highs and lows she was experiencing in hermit mode and the key realizations that were coming up during her healing journey. I told her that she needed to find ways to take care of herself during those times.

"I need to focus on myself and my healing. I know it won't be easy, but I'm ready to do the work," Haley said with a determined look in her eyes.

WHY HERMIT MODE IS NECESSARY

Imagine you've just finished a marathon. Your body is exhausted, your muscles are aching, and you're out of breath. Just as a marathon runner needs to rest and recuperate post-race, your heart and soul need to recover after the grueling experience of a damaging relationship. The intensity of relationship stress acts as a kind of emotional marathon, pushing our feelings and spirit to the limit.

Hermit mode is your body and soul's intuitive response to this stress. It's their way of signaling, "Hey, we've been through a lot. Let's take a breather." It's a necessary pause—a trauma response that ensures you give yourself the gentle care and attention you so desperately need. In essence, it's your body's way of recalibrating, trying to find its emotional and psychological equilibrium once more.

FROM HERMIT MODE TO INTENTIONAL HEALING: THE JOURNEY TO THE HEART SABBATICAL

While hermit mode offers a cocoon of safety, allowing you to rest and recalibrate after the storm, there comes a point where you might feel an inner nudge, signaling that it's time to step into deeper healing waters. This is where the heart sabbatical comes into play, beckoning you toward a more structured, intentional journey of rediscovery.

Unlike the gentle embrace of hermit mode, the heart sabbatical is more of a committed pledge—an active decision to prioritize your well-being above everything else. It's about making the conscious choice to avoid romantic entanglements for a significant period, ensuring that you're not seeking external validation to fill any voids. This is your time to bask in solitude, to listen to that inner voice, and to reconnect with the core of who you are.

The heart sabbatical encourages you to delve deep into self-reflection, nurturing your bond with yourself. By abstaining from the whirlwind of dating, you create a serene environment to rekindle old passions, invest time in hobbies, reforge bonds with friends, and embark on passion projects. It's a space where you actively work on rebuilding your self-worth without relying on another's lens to view yourself.

Yes, it won't be a walk in the park. This journey will demand determination, patience, and heaps of self-love. But the rewards? Immeasurable. You'll transition from feeling like a victim to embodying a vixen: empowered, radiant, and rooted in self-assurance. It's the ultimate step to break free from cycles of emotional chaos, and instead, build foundations based on emotional safety, genuine connection, and profound trust.

As we say goodbye to the turbulence of past relationships, let's focus on the most pivotal relationship you'll ever have—the one with yourself. The next chapter, The Heart Sabbatical, is your roadmap to just that, guiding you on how to invest in, nurture, and flourish in your own company.

4

· · · · · · · · · · ·

The Heart Sabbatical

There were days when Haley felt confident in her decision to take time off from dating and focus on herself. She enjoyed her new hobbies, solo trips, and quality time spent with her friends. But there were also days when she felt lonely and missed the comfort of being in a relationship.

In our therapy sessions, Haley talked about her journey of self-discovery and the lightbulb moments she had around her self-worth outside of a relationship. She realized that she had been using relationships as a way to validate her worth and boost her self-esteem. Now, without the distraction of a partner, she had to learn how to love and value herself outside of a relationship.

"I never realized how much I relied on my partner to make me feel good about myself," Haley said. "But now that I'm on my own, I have to learn how to be enough for myself."

I nodded in agreement. "It's a common struggle for many people, Haley. But the good news is that you're making progress by recognizing it and taking steps to change it."

Haley also talked to her friends about her journey and the lessons she was learning. They listened to and supported her, and Haley was grateful for their encouragement.

One day, while on a solo trip, Haley had a lightbulb moment about intuition. She realized that in her previous relationships, she had ignored her gut feelings and red flags because she didn't want to be alone. But now, she was learning to trust her instincts and honor her boundaries.

"I can't believe how much I ignored my intuition before," Haley said. "Now that I'm not in denial about the issues in my relationship, I can hear my intuition so much clearer. It's like a weight has been lifted."

During a particularly vivid session, Haley described a coastal weekend getaway she'd taken with Jeremy. As they were walking along the shore, watching the sun paint the sky with hues of pink and gold, she'd excitedly pointed out a particularly unique seashell. Instead of sharing her enthusiasm, Jeremy had offhandedly remarked, "You always get excited about dumb stuff! Chill, it's just a seashell!"

The comment, though seemingly benign, was soaked in condescension, making her joy feel trivial. In the past, Haley would have brushed it off, laughing nervously to diffuse the tension. But now, recalling it, she felt the sting of its subtle cruelty.

"I remember that twinge of embarrassment, like a child being scolded," she shared, a distant look in her eyes. "Back then, I just giggled and let it slide. But deep down, I felt small."

I leaned in and said, "That's your intuition, Haley. It was signaling to you that his words weren't kind. It's crucial to listen to yourself in those moments."

With a sigh of realization, Haley replied, "It's just crazy how I muted those whispers of intuition just to keep the peace. But they were trying to show me the reality all along."

As time passed, Haley continued to grow and learn from her experiences. She learned the lessons from her past relationships and how they mirrored back her own issues that she had been avoiding. She realized that by taking a break from dating, she was able to focus on herself and heal those wounds.

Haley's journey was not without its challenges, but she was grateful for the opportunity to rediscover herself and grow as a person. She learned that true happiness and fulfillment come from within, and she didn't need a relationship to feel complete.

I often remind my clients that we are social creatures, and need connections with others to thrive, like how Haley regularly leaned on her friends. However, it's also important to have a strong connection with yourself and remember that romantic relationships aren't the only sources of healing. In a world that emphasizes the importance of finding a partner and being in a relationship, it's easy to forget about the relationship you have with yourself and how healing it can be to have safe platonic relationships as well.

That's where the concept of a heart sabbatical comes in. It's a time to step back, take a break from dating, and focus on reconnecting with yourself. It's an opportunity to refocus, recalibrate, and return home to yourself. This contrasts with hermit mode, which is a smaller pause that helps you recover from the immediacy of emotional exhaustion and pain. Hermit mode is where we heal the immediate hurt. When we move to the heart sabbatical, we can do the actual work of looking inward. In this longer sanctuary of self-care, we can heal something deeper.

A heart sabbatical is the next step, like physical therapy after a surgery. It's not just about healing so that you can begin to have thriving relationships. It's more intentional, more structured. In hermit mode, you soothe and comfort your weary heart; in the heart sabbatical, you empower it. You not only tend to past wounds but also set a path forward, ensuring you have the tools and resilience to face the future with strength and clarity. In this journey, you go deeper into yourself, uncovering patterns, laying new foundations, and ensuring that you're not just recovering, but thriving. So while hermit mode holds your hand through the initial pain, the heart sabbatical guides you toward a renewed self, ready to embrace love on your terms.

By taking this time, you can learn to be comfortable in your skin, build self-worth, and hear your intuition better. The heart sabbatical is a chance to invest in the healing journey and lay the foundation for healthy relationships in the future.

WHAT EXACTLY IS A HEART SABBATICAL AND WHY YOU MIGHT NEED ONE

The heart sabbatical is a time of intentional pause, a chance to step back from the autopilot of messy relationships and take a deeper look at your role in them. It's a time to reflect on the patterns that have emerged in your relationships, both romantic and platonic, and to begin to understand the wounds and traumas that have shaped you.

By intentionally creating space for this introspection, you can begin to identify the ways in which you may have been unconsciously contributing to negative patterns in your relationships. You can also begin to develop an understanding of what you truly want and need from your future relationships, rather than simply repeating old patterns that no longer serve you.

The heart sabbatical is also an opportunity to practice self-care and self-love. It's a time to prioritize your own needs and desires, to take care of yourself in ways you may have been neglecting in your past relationships. This may include taking up new hobbies, exploring new interests, or simply taking the time to rest and rejuvenate.

While the heart sabbatical may be challenging at times, it ultimately provides you with the opportunity to become more whole, self-aware, and ready for the healthy, fulfilling relationships you deserve.

HOW THE HEART SABBATICAL WORKS

Taking a heart sabbatical allows you to step away from the chaos and drama of toxic relationships and focus on healing, self-care, and personal growth. However, it's important to establish some clear boundaries in order to make the most of your time away from relationships.

For now, put a lid on all romantic relationships, dating, and sex. Shutting down all potentials, exes, side pieces, and loose ends is necessary to avoid any distractions that might derail your progress.

This might seem difficult or even impossible, especially if

you're used to seeking validation or comfort from them, but it's crucial for giving yourself the space you need to heal and establish new ways of getting your needs met.

Additionally, some people might find it helpful to abstain from alcohol and other substances. During the sabbatical, they might realize that they've been using these to cope with the stress and turmoil of tumultuous relationships. Taking a break from substance use can help them establish healthier coping mechanisms and make better choices moving forward.

Breathe. It'll be okay. I'll be here to guide you throughout the journey.

Believe it or not, most people report enjoying the time on the sabbatical once they get past the initial fear of taking a step back. Stepping back from dating life opens up time and energy to work on creating a life that you love, and that is just for you. This might include focusing on self-care, deep introspection, healing, and reflection. I usually recommend spending four to six months honoring and re-establishing via the heart sabbatical. Many people report enjoying the time away from relationship drama so much that they extend their sabbatical even beyond four to six months.

Reconnecting with your friend group can be a helpful way to feel supported and loved during this time. Traveling and taking yourself on solo dates when possible can also help you learn to enjoy your own company and appreciate the beauty of the world around you. Finally, diving into a passion project or hobby can be a great way to rediscover your interests and connect with your authentic self. Reading several self-help books, finding a coaching program like the Inner Circle membership, and starting psychotherapy are other great ways to gain insight and support during this time.

Overall, taking a heart sabbatical can be an incredibly valuable experience. By establishing clear boundaries, you can make the most of your time away from relationships and emerge stronger, healthier, and more in touch with your true self.

UNPACKING PANDORA'S BOX ON YOUR HEART SABBATICAL

Let's return to the idea of a Pandora's box, which we introduced in Chapter 1. Taking a heart sabbatical can be a time of deep introspection and self-reflection, and one of the most important parts of this process is continuing the work of unpacking your Pandora's box. During a heart sabbatical, we have the opportunity to open this box and explore its contents in a safe and supportive environment. It might be helpful to seek the support of a licensed psychotherapist during this time to help you navigate any overwhelming emotional trauma that might show up.

One of the most powerful ways to unpack Pandora's box is by reflecting on the past and how it connects to the present. This can involve looking back at past relationships and experiences and examining how they may have shaped your patterns and behaviors in current relationships.

Keep in mind, this can be an overwhelming experience. As past traumas, memories, and patterns re-emerge, it's essential to remember that this process, while intense, is a pathway to healing.

Here's how you can navigate through:

Create a Safe Space

Unpacking Pandora's box is a bit like cleaning out an old attic; you're bound to stumble across memories and emotions that have been collecting dust for years. It can feel overwhelming, maybe even a little scary, but there's also a beauty in rediscovering those hidden parts of yourself. Now, when these forgotten traumas and emotions start to surface, it's okay to feel shaken. Breathe. Remember, they're coming up for a reason—to be acknowledged, understood, and, ultimately, healed. So create a space for yourself first, perhaps a cozy corner of your home with candles, soft music, and your favorite blanket, where you can sit with your feelings without judgment.

Seek Support

Remember, it's okay to ask for help. Whether it's confiding in a trusted friend, reaching out in a group program like my Inner Circle, or seeking guidance from a therapist, share your journey. Connecting with others who are on similar journeys can be reassuring. They offer a sense of community, understanding, and shared wisdom. Remember, you're not alone in this. Sometimes, just voicing these feelings can lighten their weight.

Journal Your Journey

Journaling can be another therapeutic outlet. When emotions bubble up, put pen to paper. Writing them out can offer clarity and a fresh perspective. It can also help you trace back patterns and recognize where they first began.

Prioritize Self-Care

As you uncover painful memories or patterns, it's okay to take breaks. This is not a race. Listen to what your body and mind need. It's okay to feel the full range of emotions that come with grieving the end of a relationship, including the root griefs— for example, grieving the father we never had, which has influenced our choice in partner. If something feels too intense, give yourself permission to step back and revisit when you're ready. This isn't just about spa days or bubble baths, but truly listening to what your heart and soul need. Maybe it's a walk in nature, or perhaps it's a dance session in your living room. Take space to reflect on the good times and the what-ifs, while also allowing yourself to process the pain, hurt, and rejection that may come with a breakup. Whatever it is, ensure you're giving yourself moments of joy and relaxation.

Practice Mindfulness and Meditation

Grounding exercises can help center you when you feel overwhelmed. Meditation, deep breathing, and even simple practices like taking walks can help manage anxiety and offer clarity. Here's one you can try, a nature-based grounding exercise:

THE TREE VISUALIZATION

ROOTS
Begin by sitting comfortably or standing with your feet firmly on the ground. Close your eyes and visualize yourself as a tall, sturdy tree. Imagine roots growing from the soles of your feet, anchoring you deep into the earth. Feel the stability and strength from these roots, holding you firmly in place.

TRUNK
Shift your focus to your body, the trunk of your tree. Just as the tree has a solid foundation that supports its branches and leaves, so does your body support your thoughts and emotions. Take a deep breath in, imagining nourishing water and minerals traveling up from your roots, feeding and energizing your entire being.

LEAVES
Picture the top of your head and your outstretched arms as branches full of vibrant leaves. As you breathe out, imagine these leaves rustling in the wind, releasing any negativity or anxiety into the atmosphere.

SUN AND AIR
Visualize the warmth of the sun caressing your leaves and the fresh air circulating around you. With every inhale, absorb this positivity. With every exhale, let go of any burdens, trusting the earth below to receive and transform them.

COMPLETION
When you feel more grounded and calm, gently wiggle your fingers and toes, bringing movement back into the body. Open your eyes slowly, carrying this feeling of stability and calmness with you.

Using the powerful imagery of nature, this exercise not only connects you with the present moment but also instills a sense of belonging and interconnectedness with the world around you. It serves as a gentle reminder of nature's cycles, where every element has its place, purpose, and time to flourish.

AFFIRMATIONS AND SELF-COMPASSION

Reminding yourself of your worth and practicing self-compassion is crucial. Use affirmations to reinforce positive beliefs about yourself. Forgive your past self and embrace your present self, recognizing the strength in your journey.

ENGAGING IN PASSION PROJECTS

Reconnect with hobbies and activities that make you feel alive and happy. They can act as a wonderful distraction, giving you positive outlets when things feel heavy.

Remember, the heart sabbatical is about deepening your connection to yourself. As you unpack Pandora's box, you're not just confronting the past but actively paving the way for a future filled with understanding, self-love, and healthier relational patterns. Each challenge faced and memory processed takes you a step closer to the empowered, resilient self you're cultivating.

By understanding the roots of our patterns and behaviors, we can begin to make changes and break free from unhealthy cycles. This can lead to us being able to acknowledge and address our own red flags.

Note: I don't refer to having unresolved trauma as "red flags" because that furthers the stigma around getting help to address them. I refer to dysfunctional, harmful behavior as red flags: triangulation, gaslighting, emotional/verbal/physical abuse, intentionally confusing language, circular arguments, ghosting, stonewalling, etc.

OWNING YOUR RED FLAGS

It's common to unconsciously choose partners and situations based on unresolved emotional wounds from your past. This is due to a psychological phenomenon called *repetitive compulsion*, where you unconsciously seek out and repeat events that are connected to unresolved emotional pain. This can make it difficult to see that you're unconsciously choosing codependent relationships.

When we're in these situations, our brains are wired to seek out what's familiar, even if it's not safe or healthy. In navigating life, we often find solace in what feels familiar, like a favorite old song. This isn't just nostalgia; it's a deep-seated drive to make sense of past experiences, particularly those that may have hurt us.

For instance, if you grew up with a parent who had addiction issues, you might unconsciously seek out a partner with the same struggles. You might feel like you have to take care of them in order to win their love and attention, repeating the same pattern you witnessed in childhood. It's as if a part of you believes that by helping this person, you can somehow "rewrite" or "master" the pain from your past.

This journey, while challenging, can also be an invitation to heal wounds and patterns we didn't even know were still open. Every twist and turn, while sometimes perplexing, offers a chance to better understand ourselves and our story.

The good news is that once you become aware of this pattern, you can take steps to heal. This is where a heart sabbatical comes in. By taking time away from painful relationships, you can reflect on your past wounds and learn to heal them. This self-awareness can help you make better choices in future relationships, leading to greater emotional depth, maturity, and intelligence.

For instance, you might realize that you're experiencing hypervigilance and high reactivity in your current relationship because of past betrayals and infidelity in a previous relationship. By taking time for self-reflection during a heart sabbatical, you can learn to self-soothe and separate your past from your present. This can help you avoid sabotaging your current relationship and build healthier, more fulfilling connections in the future.

Taking this a step further, imagine growing up in a household where one of your parents was a dominant figure, always needing to have the last word or be in control. That kind of upbringing can leave subtle imprints on your heart and mind. As you navigate through life, you might find yourself constantly seeking approval in your romantic relationships, feeling the need to always say "yes" even when you want to say "no." In professional settings, you might constantly second-guess your decisions, waiting for validation before taking action. In platonic friendships, you might avoid conflicts, fearing that asserting yourself might lead to rejection or abandonment.

Dedicating time for a heart sabbatical lets you gently delve into these patterns. It offers you a serene space to recognize that your eager-to-please attitude or hesitation to speak up is rooted in that early familial dynamic. With awareness and self-compassion, you can start to craft a new narrative for yourself—one where you acknowledge your worth and learn to stand firm in your beliefs and desires. This transformative journey not only enhances your personal relationships but also strengthens your voice in the broader tapestry of life, from boardroom conversations to coffee shop chats with friends.

Why is it important to heal our nervous systems after ending traumatic relationships? The body is incredible and can handle high levels of stress, but you were never meant to live in a constant state of survival mode. Unfortunately, toxic relationships can put you in that mode, adding to the stress you may already be dealing with from unresolved trauma, money issues, and imbalances in your diet, exercise, and self-care. That's why it's so important to prioritize healing your nervous system.

When you're in survival mode, your body's fight-or-flight response kicks in, releasing stress hormones like cortisol and adrenaline. Over time, this can have a detrimental impact on your physical and mental health. But by taking the time to re-set our nervous system, we can begin to self-soothe and create a self-care regimen that helps us better manage stress.

It's common for people who experienced childhood trauma or grew up in environments where stress was the norm to strug-gle with high levels of anxiety and tension as adults. They may even find themselves in relationships that replicate the same patterns of conflict and tension they experienced growing up. But just because you survived something in your past doesn't mean it's healthy or normal to continue living in a state of constant stress.

By taking the time to heal your nervous system, you can begin to recalibrate and reset. This means not only addressing the effects of toxic relationships but also acknowledging and working through your own unresolved trauma and stressors. It's about creating a new normal for yourself where you prioritize self-care and establish healthy boundaries in your relationships. During this time, you might find yourself sleeping more than usual as your body resets your nervous system. Ultimately, the goal is to live a life that feels safe, peaceful, and nourishing to the mind, body, and soul.

The Red Flag Reflection Exercise

Often, we get so caught up in identifying the red flags in others that we overlook our own. This exercise grounds us, shining a light on those personal patterns that might be hold-ing us back.

MATERIALS NEEDED:

- A quiet space
- A journal or piece of paper
- Your favorite pen

RED FLAG REFLECTION EXERCISE	
REVISIT PAST RELATIONSHIPS	Begin by listing significant relationships or situationships in your life.
IDENTIFY PATTERNS	For each relationship, jot down moments when you felt uneasy or ignored your intuition. These are potential red flags. Were there any recurring themes?
REFLECT ON YOUR ROLE	Ask yourself, "In what way did I respond to these flags? Did I address them, ignore them, or justify them?" Be honest but gentle with yourself.
UNDERSTAND YOUR "WHY"	Dive deep into the "why" behind your reactions. Was it fear of abandonment? A desire to please? A fear of confrontation?
ENVISION HEALTHIER RESPONSES	For each identified pattern or flag, jot down a healthier way to respond. For example, if you often ignore problems hoping they'll go away, perhaps you could choose to communicate openly about them in the future.

As you dive into this exercise, remember that this isn't about beating yourself up. It's about getting to know yourself a bit better, like catching up with an old friend. This journey is all about understanding, not criticizing. By spotting these personal warning signs and getting the scoop on where they come from, you're paving a path toward some real, heartfelt growth. And trust me, that's a pretty beautiful thing.

TRUSTING YOUR
INTUITION & REFUSING DENIAL

When you experience trauma in a relationship, it can shake you to your core. It's like a storm that passes through, leaving you with a mess to clean up. Sometimes, in order to pick up the pieces and move on, you might engage in denial, pretending everything is okay when it's not. It's a coping mechanism, a way to survive the impact of the trauma.

But denial comes at a cost. It dampens your intuition, the inner voice that guides you toward what's right and away from what's wrong. And the more you deny your trauma, the more you lose touch with your intuition. It's like a fog that settles over you, making it hard to see clearly.

When you can tap into your intuition, you can sense red flags before the first date. You can recognize when something doesn't feel right, even if you can't put your finger on why. Pay attention and check in with yourself regularly throughout any interaction; ask yourself if what's being said or done feels right for you. If something doesn't feel right, then you can act accordingly. And that can save you from a lot of heartache down the road.

Once again, tapping into your Pandora's box of old, shameful feelings and memories you tried to put aside can be useful here. Sorting through your past can be an important first step in reconnecting with your intuition. Here are some questions you can ask yourself during this process:

- How does your Pandora's box show up in your life?
- What patterns keep repeating themselves in your relationships?
- How did you feel about your past as a child or when it was happening?
- How does this compare to what you now think and feel about it as an adult?
- What lessons do you need to learn from patterns that have shown up in your relationships?
- What's the attachment style of the people you seem to attract?
- In contrast, how would a secure partner, high in integrity and comfortable in their identity, in contrast, treat you?
- How would you respond to a secure partner in the past, and how does that compare to how you know you should respond now?

COMING HOME TO OURSELVES BY STARTING THE INNER WORK

Embarking on a journey through inner child healing, ego development, and shadow discovery is like renovating an old home that's seen its fair share of storms. A heart sabbatical is the perfect time to roll up our sleeves and get to work on the renovations. Each aspect, from repairing the foundation to polishing the windows, offers a step closer to a sanctuary that truly feels like home. I'll cover the steps briefly here, and we'll dive even deeper in Part 2.

Inner Child Healing

The first layer we meet is our inner child. Think of this as the foundation of a house; our childhood memories and feelings are the bricks and mortar. Starting our healing journey here is like fixing any cracks in that foundation. *It's crucial to tend to this layer first,* as these early wounds can dictate a lot of our subconscious reactions, triggers, and behaviors in adulthood. Healing the inner child means mending our foundational cracks by revisiting those moments of pain, neglect, or misunderstanding, and offering ourselves the love, attention, and care we've been yearning for.

Ego Work

Delving deeper, we find the ego, which is akin to the walls of our emotional home. While our inner child might hide in the foundation after facing trauma, our ego responds by putting up thick curtains and bolted doors. In codependent or toxic relationships, this might look like being overly reactive when a partner shares concerns, seeing it as criticism instead of healthy communication. It's the urge to cling tighter, fearing abandonment amid unrequited love, or to erect emotional walls to avoid getting hurt. Ego work, then, is about gently drawing back those heavy curtains, lowering the walls, and unlocking the doors. It's an invitation to let love, connection, and vulnerability shine through, paving the way for deeper connections.

Shadow Work

Venturing to the attic and basement of our emotional home, we meet our shadow. While our inner child leaves imprints on the foundation, and our ego bolsters the walls, our shadow lurks in the less frequented spaces of our emotional home. In the context of toxic or codependent relationships, the shadow is those deep-seated fears and insecurities we'd rather not admit, or the patterns we unknowingly repeat. It's the jealousy we feel but don't voice, the guilt we bury, or the unworthiness we sometimes feel but can't pinpoint why.

Shadow work is like turning on the light in these dim spaces, dusting off old boxes, and understanding their contents. It involves exploring and embracing the parts of ourselves that we have abandoned, repressed, or denied. These can be aspects of our personalities that we don't want to acknowledge, such as anger, jealousy, or fear. When we ignore or suppress these parts of ourselves, they can manifest in destructive ways, such as in toxic relationships. Shadow work is about facing and integrating every hidden aspect influencing our relationships, ensuring our emotional home is whole, healthy, and solid, from basement to rooftop.

Let's circle back to Haley from earlier in this chapter. As a child, her parents were often so caught up in their own issues that they seemed to overlook her needs. She felt like she was constantly in the shadows, especially with her younger sister getting all of their attention. This dynamic only amplified Haley's feelings of invisibility. You see, her sister, always the bubbly one, naturally drew the spotlight and the coveted attention of her parents. It's as if Haley's own light dimmed in comparison. She often wondered what it would take to be seen, to have a moment where she wasn't just the older sister in the background.

In the context of shadow work, this aspect of Haley's life represents a significant shadow—those unacknowledged parts of herself that were never nurtured. Her feelings of being overlooked in favor of her sister created a deep-rooted belief that she was less worthy of attention and love. This belief, buried in her shadow, has continued to influence her actions and self-perception into adulthood.

It's clear now that her parents never really grasped how much Haley craved their attention and validation. Today, this longing hasn't faded. Haley often finds herself going above and beyond in her job, hoping for the acknowledgment she missed out on growing up.

These childhood experiences can shape our adult responses in myriad ways. They can manifest as persistent feelings of self-doubt, toxic shame, low self-esteem, and relentless negative self-talk. Inner child work coupled with shadow work aims to address these manifestations at their core. It involves not only identifying but also embracing and integrating these deeply ingrained patterns into a more holistic understanding of the self. Through this conscientious process, Haley can work toward releasing these shadows, stepping out of her sister's light, and finding her own place in the sun.

So, what does this work look like in action?

INNER CHILD WORK WHILE ON A HEART SABBATICAL

In this first pillar of healing, you'll learn how to create a strong foundation of self-love and self-worth that sets the stage for healing the relationship you have with yourself. Since inner child work focuses on early childhood traumas, you'll be identifying and healing the wounds you experienced during your childhood. These often become the root cause of our behavior and thought patterns as adults. Your inner child is the part of you that holds on to your emotions and memories from youth. Ignoring or suppressing them can create challenges in choosing, forming, *and maintaining* healthy relationships.

By connecting with your inner child, you learn to give this part of yourself the love, validation, and connection you've been missing. You'll also learn how to release the hold that past wounds have on your present relationships.

Identify Patterns

Begin by looking at your emotional triggers. Are there recurring themes or events that create strong emotional reactions? For Haley, feedback, especially when it's negative, can be a painful trigger. She will want to pay attention to this and work to soothe her inner child who still feels invalidated when she doesn't feel acknowledged for her efforts. Her triggers are in response to earlier childhood events that left her feeling "not good enough," and because these feelings remained unresolved, they're like emotional landmines waiting for contact to go off.

Connect with Your Inner Child

Dedicate quiet moments to visualizing and engaging with your younger self. It's about truly listening to this past version of you, acknowledging their emotions and experiences. Haley might envision being in the room with her younger self, comforting her and reassuring her of her worth and importance while in the midst of feeling invalidated and unacknowledged. Engage in activities that resonate with your inner child. This could be something as whimsical as coloring or as grounding as a walk in nature. For Haley, reconnecting with her love for painting—a hobby she'd forgotten about over the years—was therapeutic, as were other activities grounded in play that she enjoyed as a child.

Take your time and allow yourself the space to identify your patterns, connect with the parts of yourself that felt neglected, hurt, and abandoned, and then re-engage in activities you loved but maybe don't get to do enough as an adult. This will set the stage for the rest of your healing journey. By giving light to these areas, we open doors to healthier relationships with others and ourselves.

The ego can feel like an enigmatic part of our psyche. It plays such a huge role in how we interact with others, yet we often don't understand it. Do we follow the advice of the monks on a hill and let the ego die, or do we sit with it, observing how it shows up in an effort to understand how it has developed in response to trauma? On one hand, it embodies the childlike innocence of egocentrism. Remember when as children, we believed the world revolved around us? That if it rained on our parade, the skies were crying with us? This is the ego in its purest form.

On the other hand, unresolved traumas and toxic experiences can cause the ego to be stunted in this stage, preventing it from maturing healthily.

For Haley, childhood overshadowing left her ego in a tender state. As she grew older, instead of her ego maturing, the unresolved pain caused it to remain as it was—self-centered and easily hurt. When her partner would have a bad day, her immediate thought would be, "Did I do something wrong?" It was not about empathizing with him; it was more about her ego fearing blame. Similarly, she found herself attracted to distant relationships, chasing unrequited love. Not because it was true affection, but because her ego, in its desperate bid to avoid further rejection, became obsessed with winning their heart in order to prove that she was "good enough."

TENDING TO THE EGO ON A HEART SABBATICAL

By understanding and tending to our ego, we can move past its childlike, impetuous responses and foster a more mature and balanced sense of self. Here are a few steps to do this, but again, we'll go deeper in Part 2. This is just a taste for the beginning of your heart sabbatical.

Awareness

Pay attention to your thoughts and internal reactions to daily events. What are some recurring themes? Are you struggling with obsessive, intrusive thoughts about a situation? Are those thoughts grounded in control, avoidance, or another defense mechanism? Pay attention to what triggers these negative, unhelpful thoughts. Journaling about this can be a helpful way to keep a record.

Understand the Origins

Reflect on past experiences that might have caused this stunting of your emotional maturity. For Haley, her constant need for validation stems from the overshadowing during her formative years. She may now realize that feeling triggered if her employee evaluation doesn't have stellar compliments results from her bruised ego, which developed in response to rarely feeling validated growing up. Her goal here is to self-soothe amid thoughts that she will have to overfunction at work and in her romantic relationships in order to feel validated. She'll also work on self-validation, setting boundaries around workplace achievements and external feedback to understand that she is good enough regardless of the feedback she receives. The feedback is just that: feedback. Not an indication of her worth.

Engage in Ego-Check Exercises

Use the "Pause and Reflect" technique. When you're about to react, take a moment to ask, "Is this my true self responding, or is it my ego acting out of past hurts?" This can help temper ego-driven reactions and guide you toward a balanced, mature self-perception.

SHADOW WORK DURING A HEART SABBATICAL

Shadow work is like finally opening up that old photo album. Some memories might be awkward or painful, but they're all part of your story. By understanding and integrating them, we get a richer, more honest picture of ourselves.

Meet the Hidden Guests

Think of your shadow as those old toys you tucked away in the attic. They're the parts of you that got boxed up because they didn't quite fit your present-day image. It's time to climb up, dust off those boxes, and meet them again.

Connect the Dots

As you discover these tucked-away parts, you might remember why they were hidden in the first place. For Haley, she might reflect on the times she silently resented her sister. That, coupled with entertaining harsh self-talk telling herself that she will never be good enough while also resenting her sister for being able to secure her parents' attention and validation. Reflecting on these parts helps Haley make sense of the underlying resentment preventing her from having a close relationship with her sister.

The "Embrace, Don't Erase" Technique

Instead of shoving these parts back into the dark, let's give them a little spotlight. Ask, "What are they trying to tell me?" Welcoming them can offer a fuller, more rounded sense of self.

Together, inner child work, ego work, and shadow work provide a powerful framework for healing and recalibrating the relationship you have with yourself. By identifying and healing your inner wounds, developing a healthier sense of self, and embracing all aspects of yourself, you can break free from the patterns that hold you back and create healthier, more fulfilling relationships.

Let's focus on inner child work for now, as ego and shadow work will be discussed in deeper detail in the following section. There are different approaches to inner child work, but they all share a common goal: to help you connect with your inner child and provide the nurturing and support that you may have missed out on in childhood. Some techniques that aid our healing of the inner child include journaling, visualization, meditation, and talking to your inner child.

Journaling is a powerful tool for inner child work. By writing down your thoughts and feelings, you can identify the patterns and beliefs that may be holding you back. You can also use journaling to communicate with your inner child, asking them what they need and how you can support them. Here are a few questions to get you started:

Revisiting Memories: Think back to a childhood moment when you felt intense emotion (whether happiness,

sadness, fear, or excitement). Describe the scene in detail.
Who was there? What happened? How did it make you
feel then, and how does it make you feel now?

Messages from the Past: What messages or beliefs did you
internalize from your parents, caregivers, or other significant figures from your childhood? How have these
messages influenced your decisions, self-worth, and
relationships in adulthood?

Conversations with the Younger You: If you could have a
heart-to-heart conversation with your younger self, what
would you say? What would they say back to you? What
advice, comfort, or perspective would you offer them?

Visualization involves creating a mental image of your inner child and imagining yourself providing the support and
love that they need in the present moment. You can also visualize yourself going back in time to soothe and reassure your
inner child during a time when they needed it the most.

Meditation is another effective tool in inner child work
that plays a pivotal role in inner child healing. Sitting in silence, focusing intently on your breath, does several transformative things:

Calms Mind Chatter: Our minds are often filled with
a cacophony of thoughts, memories, and emotions.
Meditation helps quiet this internal noise, making it
easier to tune into the deeper, often suppressed parts of
ourselves.

Regulates the Body's Stress Response: Deep, focused

breathing activates our parasympathetic nervous system—the part responsible for calming the body and mind. This physiological response creates a relaxed environment, facilitating a deeper emotional connection to our inner child.

Creates a Safe Emotional Environment: In the tranquility of meditation, we can visualize a safe space where our inner child feels protected and heard. This mental sanctum allows for vulnerable memories and emotions to surface without the fear of judgment or external disturbances.

Enhances Self-Awareness: Meditation sharpens our introspective abilities, enabling us to recognize patterns, feelings, and reactions that might stem from childhood experiences. With this awareness, we can more effectively address and nurture those wounded parts.

By merging the calming effects on the mind and body with focused introspection, meditation creates a nurturing environment where our inner child can step forward, be acknowledged, and begin the healing journey.

Soothing self-talk is also an important aspect of inner child work. By addressing your inner child directly and acknowledging their pain and needs, you can begin to repair the relationship you have with yourself. Here are a few examples of soothing self-talk:

"It makes sense that you feel this way."
"You did the best you could back then. I'm proud of you."

"I love you, and I'm here now."
"It wasn't your fault. I'll protect you now."
"I'm listening. Tell me how you feel, and we'll work through it
together."
"You are safe now. I won't let anyone hurt you anymore."
"I apologize for not being there for you earlier. Let's reconnect."
"You are not alone anymore. We're in this together."

Self-reflection is needed for the task of recognizing the emotional triggers that stem from childhood experiences. This can be uncomfortable, but it is a crucial step in healing your inner child. It's not always a comfortable journey, but it can be a game-changer once you realize how your triggers have been running your emotional show.

1. **Identify Emotional Triggers:** Begin by carrying a small notebook with you or using a notes app on your phone. Whenever you notice a strong emotional reaction to a situation, jot it down. It might be a feeling of intense anxiety when someone is late or an overwhelming sadness when you feel excluded from a group.
2. **Reflect on the Origin:** Set aside quiet time each week to review these triggers. Ask yourself, "When was the first time I felt this way?" or "Does this remind me of something in my past?" Often, you'll find that current reactions are magnified by past experiences.
3. **Seek Support:** Discussing these triggers with a trusted friend, family member, or therapist can be invaluable. They can offer a fresh perspective and may help you see

patterns you weren't aware of. If you decide to discuss it with someone, choose a person who's empathetic and non-judgmental.

4. **Accountability Partner:** Having someone who knows about your journey can be beneficial. They can gently point out when they notice a trigger reaction in you, allowing you to catch and address it sooner.

5. **Affirmations and Reassurance:** Whenever you recognize a trigger, offer words of comfort to your inner child. It could be as simple as whispering to yourself, "It's okay, I'm here for you now."

6. **Continue the Dialogue:** Consider setting aside a few minutes each day for "inner child time." This can be a moment where you mentally check in with your younger self, ask how they're feeling, and offer reassurance.

By identifying and reflecting on these emotional triggers, and with the help of supportive figures in your life, you can start to unpack and heal the childhood wounds they're connected to. For example, if you grapple with abandonment issues today, it might be tied back to earlier times in your life when you felt left behind or overlooked. By acknowledging and addressing these root causes, you take a big step toward healing.

Creating a Safe Space

Another task is creating a safe and nurturing space for your inner child to express themselves. Creating a dedicated, safe environment for self-exploration is fundamental. This isn't just about mental spaces, but also physical and emotional ones.

- **Physical Space:** Choose a location where you feel at ease and undisturbed. This could be a cozy corner of your bedroom, a quiet spot in a park, or even a dedicated space in your home filled with items that evoke comfort and warmth. Here are some suggestions:
  - Soft blankets or cushions
  - Gentle lighting or candles
  - Favorite childhood toys or pictures
- **Digital Detox:** Before entering this space, consider taking a digital detox. Switch off your phone or put it on airplane mode to ensure there are no interruptions.
- **Mental Preparation:** Before diving into deeper work, take a few moments to ground yourself. This might involve taking deep breaths, listening to calming music, or practicing a brief meditation.
- **Setting Intentions:** Before each session, set clear intentions. It might be something like, "Today, I want to write a letter to the part of me that felt ignored," or "Today, I will explore why I feel anxious in crowds."

Emotional Safety

Recognize that exploring your inner child can bring up potent emotions. Have a self-care plan ready for afterward. This might include:

- A soothing activity like reading a favorite book or taking a bath
- Talking to a trusted friend or family member
- Listening to your favorite songs
- Cooking your favorite meal

Remember, the objective is to make your inner child feel valued, heard, and protected. By establishing a specific, comforting space and routine, you signal to that part of yourself that they are worth this time, attention, and love.

Going back to our past and giving our inner child the love they missed out on can change the trajectory of our lives. Through inner child work, you start to navigate challenges with a deeper sense of understanding. This doesn't just make you stronger emotionally; it also allows you to connect with others more authentically. By doing this, we lay the groundwork for richer, more meaningful relationships and a life filled with greater compassion for ourselves and those around us.

FROM CODEPENDENT LOVE TO HEALTHY LOVE

First, I want you to know that it is very possible to shift and heal codependent patterns into healthy relationships. As we heal and grow, learning to love ourselves and others in new ways can stir up conflicting emotions. This is where the journey may feel difficult, as it forces you to look at patterns that have largely allowed you to get your emotional needs met by seeking approval, love, affection, attention, and, for some, control.

Codependency often involves trying to control others covertly, overtly, consciously, or unconsciously in order to feel loved, valued, and accepted. By focusing all their energy on another person, codependents are able to avoid doing their own inner work. This is a destructive pattern that keeps people stuck in unhealthy relationships and prevents them from experiencing genuine connection and love.

It is absolutely possible to shift from codependent love to healthy love, but it takes time, self-awareness, introspection, and a willingness to take personal responsibility and accountability for your actions and expectations.

You will have to let go of the need to control others and instead focus on being in control of yourself. This may involve setting healthy boundaries, communicating effectively, and allowing others to be themselves without trying to change them.

As you navigate this journey, it is important to ask yourself tough questions about your expectations, your reactions, and your willingness to let go of codependency.

Some helpful questions to ask yourself might be:

- Are you willing to pause and think before you react?
- Are you ready to give up toxic codependent patterns and embrace the path to becoming the best version of yourself?
- What are some of your expectations that are grounded in codependency and control?

- How willing are you to pause and think about your response before reacting?
- Are you OK with accepting people as they are and then deciding if it works for you?
- How can you utilize consequential thinking so that you don't self-sabotage your healing journey?

So, after diving into these thought-provoking questions, what's the next step for you? Your answers to these questions will be a part of your personal roadmap to self-discovery and improvement. Instead of getting caught up in trying to control others, you can put your energy into making some real changes in your life. Here's how you can turn these insights into action:

Set Some Goals: Take those insights and turn them into practical goals for yourself. What are some concrete steps you can take to become the best version of yourself? Write them down.

Pause and Breathe: Remember to hit the pause button before reacting. This simple act of mindfulness can help you respond to situations more calmly and wisely.

Lean on Support: It's perfectly okay to seek support from a therapist, counselor, or even friends who understand your journey. They can provide guidance and a listening ear.

Keep Checking In: Make it a habit to check in with yourself regularly. Are you sticking to your goals? Are you shedding those codependent patterns? What's working and what needs adjustment?

Celebrate Small Wins: Don't forget to celebrate your victories along the way, no matter how small. Each step you take is a step closer to your best self.

As you embark on this journey, remember it's all about you, your growth, and your path to becoming the best version of yourself. Don't let the need to control others sidetrack you from this incredible journey of self-discovery and improvement.

SOMATIC WORK

Somatic work can be a powerful tool to implement while on your heart sabbatical. At its core, somatic work is an approach that focuses on the connection between the mind and the body, specifically how our bodies hold on to and process emotions and trauma. Imagine it as a bridge that links our physical experiences to our emotional ones.

When you are embarking on a healing journey after a toxic relationship, you must understand that the pain and trauma you experienced has left an imprint on your body. These imprints manifest in ways you may not be aware of, such as muscle tension, headaches, digestive issues, and shallow breathing. This is why somatic work is crucial in healing. By learning to regulate your nervous system and manage emotional triggers, you can begin to connect with your body and access its innate wisdom.

One important aspect of somatic work is learning to self-regulate. This means understanding how your body responds to stress, and learning tools to calm yourself down when triggered. This may include practices like deep breathing, meditation, yoga, or other forms of movement that help you connect with your body.

Another important aspect of somatic work is coping with and managing emotional triggers. You must learn to identify your triggers and how they manifest in your body. This means developing a deeper understanding of your emotional landscape and how it affects your physical well-being. With this knowledge, you can begin to cultivate practices that support you in managing your triggers when they arise.

Here are some examples:

Tightness in the Chest: Imagine you're in a meeting, and a colleague interrupts you. Suddenly, you feel a tightness in your chest. This could be an emotional trigger from past experiences when you felt unheard or invalidated. The tightness is a physical manifestation of those feelings.

Butterflies in the Stomach: Before giving a public speech or presentation, you might feel "butterflies" in your stomach. This could be tied to a past experience when you felt judged or embarrassed in front of a crowd.

Increased Heart Rate: Perhaps you're watching a movie, and a particular scene reminds you of a traumatic event. Your heart rate might increase, and you could start sweating. This is your body's fight-or-flight response to a remembered trauma.

Feeling "Frozen" or Numb: Sometimes, in stressful situations, you might feel unable to move or think clearly.

This could be a response tied to past experiences when
you felt trapped or helpless.

With this understanding, you can begin to cultivate practices that support you in managing your triggers:

Deep Breathing: When you recognize a trigger and the associated physical response, take a few deep breaths. This
helps calm the nervous system and gives you a moment
to reflect.

Grounding Techniques: Engage with your five senses. Feel
the texture of an object, listen to ambient sounds, or
focus on your breathing. Grounding helps you return
to the present moment.

Safe Spaces: Identify safe spaces where you can retreat and
collect yourself. It could be a quiet room, a park, or
even just stepping outside for fresh air.

Seek Support: Talk to someone you trust about your triggers. Sometimes, simply vocalizing your feelings helps
in understanding and managing them.

Therapeutic Modalities: Consider techniques like EMDR
(Eye Movement Desensitization and Reprocessing) or
trauma-informed yoga, which specifically address the
physical manifestations of emotional triggers.

By marrying the understanding of your emotional landscape with the physical manifestations of triggers, you're better
equipped to navigate the complexities of your well-being.

YOUR HAPPY CHEMICALS

Part of forging a connection between the mind and the body involves finding ways to hack your "happy chemicals." This means engaging in activities that promote the release of feel-good chemicals in the brain, such as dopamine and serotonin. Examples of these include exercise, spending time in nature, or engaging in creative pursuits.

When you experience trauma, your happy neurotransmitters can take a hit. However, there are ways to hack into each of these neurotransmitters to help you feel good and increase your emotional resilience.

- **Serotonin** is a neurotransmitter that is responsible for feelings of happiness and well-being. One way to boost serotonin levels is through exposure to sunlight. Spending time outside in nature, even just for a few minutes a day, can do wonders for your mood. Another way to boost serotonin is through exercise. Even moderate physical activity, like a brisk walk, can help elevate your mood and increase serotonin levels.
- **Dopamine** is a neurotransmitter that is associated with reward and pleasure. One way to boost dopamine is to set achievable goals and reward yourself when you meet them. This can be as simple as treating yourself to a favorite snack or taking a break to watch an episode of your favorite show after finishing a task. Engaging in activities that bring you pleasure, such as listening

to music or dancing, can also help boost dopamine
levels.

- **Endorphins** are neurotransmitters that are associated
  with pain relief and pleasure. One way to boost endorphins is through exercise. Vigorous physical activity, like
  running or weight lifting, can help release endorphins
  and make you feel good. Laughter is also a great way to
  release endorphins. Watching a funny movie, reading
  a humorous book, or spending time with friends who
  make you laugh can all help boost endorphin levels.

- **Oxytocin** is a neurotransmitter that is associated with
  bonding and social connection. One way to boost oxytocin is through physical touch. Hugging, cuddling, and
  even holding hands with someone you care about can
  release oxytocin and make you feel connected. Engaging
  in acts of kindness, such as volunteering or doing something nice for someone else, can also help boost oxytocin
  levels.

Hacking your happy neurotransmitters can be a powerful
tool in your healing journey after a toxic relationship. These
activities not only make you feel good in the moment, but also
help you build emotional resilience and increase your overall
sense of well-being. This approach is often effective because
your ex may have been a significant source of happiness for
you in the past, and perhaps you relied on them as one of your
primary sources of joy. With their absence, it becomes crucial
to recalibrate by discovering and embracing other sources of
positive emotions in your life. Through this you can begin to

cultivate a more diverse range of happy chemicals, ultimately leading to a life that feels grounded, safe, and connected.

In reconnecting with your body, you can increase your intuition and learn to differentiate between intuition and fear. By developing a deep connection with your physical self, you can tap into your inner wisdom and make better decisions in relationships.

Remember, healing is a journey that requires patience, compassion, and dedication. By committing to somatic work, you will learn to reconnect with your body and access the wisdom and intuition that lies within.

STANDARDS, DEAL BREAKERS, CORE VALUES, AND BOUNDARIES

In counseling my clients from codependency to healthy relationships, I focus on four key elements: standards, deal breakers, core values, and boundaries. Let's dive into each of these.

Standards

Standards are the expectations you have for yourself and your partner in a relationship. They encompass the qualities and behaviors you value. Identifying your standards helps you understand what you want and need in a relationship, creating a benchmark for what you will accept and what you won't. Examples include honesty, respect, loyalty, kindness, and effective communication. Standards empower you to make informed choices about your partner and ensure your relationship aligns with your values.

Deal Breakers

Deal breakers are the non-negotiables in a relationship, the things you cannot tolerate. These are aspects so important that they warrant ending a relationship if they are not met. Examples may include cheating, abuse, addiction, or a lack of respect. Deal breakers protect your mental, emotional, and physical well-being and preserve your self-respect and self-worth.

Core Values

Core values are the guiding principles that define who you are, what you stand for, and what you believe in. They encompass aspects of life that are deeply significant to you, such as family, spirituality, education, or personal growth. Core values provide a moral compass, helping you stay true to yourself and your beliefs. They aid in decision-making, ensuring your actions and choices align with your life's purpose and goals.

Some examples include:

Certainty: Certainty is about having confidence and
   clarity in your relationship. You should feel sure about
   your partner's feelings and commitment to the relationship. If you are uncertain or unclear about where

you stand with your partner, it can create anxiety and doubt, which can be detrimental to the health of the relationship.

Clarity: Clarity is about being clear and direct in your communication. You should be able to express your thoughts and feelings in a way that is understood by your partner, and vice versa. Avoidance of issues or being vague can lead to misunderstandings and frustration, so it's important to be clear with your words and actions.

Commitment: Commitment is about being dedicated and invested in the relationship. It means making an effort to prioritize the relationship and to work through challenges and obstacles that may arise. A lack of commitment can lead to instability and insecurity in the relationship.

Communication: Good communication is crucial for a healthy relationship. It means actively listening to your partner, expressing your own thoughts and feelings, and finding ways to resolve conflicts and solve problems together. Communication helps foster understanding and strengthen emotional bonds.

Compromise: Compromise is a necessary value in any relationship. It means finding common ground, negotiating differences, and making mutual sacrifices for the benefit of the partnership. Compromise helps create a sense of teamwork and collaboration, and fosters feelings of respect and appreciation.

Consistency: Consistency is about being reliable and predictable in your actions and behavior. In a healthy relationship, you want to be able to count on your partner to be there for you when you need them, and for them to follow through on their promises. Consistency helps build trust and stability.

Emotional Safety: Emotional safety is about feeling secure and protected in the relationship. You should feel comfortable expressing yourself and being vulnerable with your partner without fear of being rejected or ridiculed. Emotional safety is necessary for building deep connections and trust in the relationship.

Emotional Security: Emotional security is about feeling confident and assured in your partner's love and commitment. It means feeling safe and secure in the knowledge that your partner values and cares for you. Emotional security helps create a stable and supportive environment that is essential for the health of the relationship.

Empathy: Empathy is an important value in any healthy relationship. It means being able to understand and share your partner's feelings and experiences, and to respond with compassion and support. Empathy helps create a sense of connection and intimacy, and fosters feelings of closeness and understanding.

Honesty: Honesty is a cornerstone of healthy relationships. It means being truthful and transparent in all your communications, and being open and upfront about your thoughts, feelings, and actions. Honesty creates trust and builds strong foundations for deeper connections.

Respect: Respect is an essential value in any healthy relationship. It means treating your partner with kindness, consideration, and empathy, and valuing their opinions, beliefs, and feelings. When partners show mutual respect, they are able to create an environment of support and validation.

Responsibility: Responsibility is a crucial value in any healthy relationship. It means taking accountability for your own actions, being reliable and dependable, and being willing to take care of your partner when they need support. Responsibility helps create a sense of stability and security, and fosters feelings of trust and respect.

Trust: Trust is a vital component of any relationship. It means having confidence in your partner, knowing that they will keep their promises and act in your best interest. Trust helps create a sense of security and stability, which is necessary for a healthy relationship.

Take some time alone to think about what you need in a relationship and why these values are important to you. These could range from things like respect, honesty, and loyalty to understanding, communication, and compassion. Once you have identified your core values, take the time to write them down and reflect on what they mean for you personally.

Boundaries

Setting boundaries is like drawing a line in the sand, defining what is and isn't acceptable in your relationships. A boundary is not an ultimatum or a punishment, and it's not a way of manipulating someone into behaving the way we want them to. Instead, it's a clear and compassionate expression of our needs and limits, which can help us navigate our relationships in a way that's respectful and authentic.

Boundaries are crucial for maintaining healthy connections with others. They can take various forms, such as emotional (expressing your feelings), physical (personal space), and relating to time (allocating time for yourself). Implementing boundaries is an act of self-preservation and self-respect. By communicating your needs and limits clearly, you build trust and respect in your relationships.

What does it look like for you when those boundaries are crossed? Start by determining what your boundaries should be in any type of relationship so you can recognize when they are being broken or disregarded. Setting clear boundaries will help protect your emotional safety within any relationship, whether platonic or romantic, as well as help you get closer to embodying your core values around healthy relationships.

Protecting your emotional well-being means identifying the relationships that cause harm—whether familial, romantic, professional, or platonic—and establishing healthy boundaries. This may involve maintaining distance, terminating relationships, or simply speaking up when someone crosses your boundaries.

The re-parenting process is about nurturing and taking care of your inner child. Your inner child may be wounded from past traumas and rejections, and it's important to acknowledge and tend to those wounds. Re-parenting them involves redirecting your thoughts and feelings when you're feeling rejected and abandoned to soothing self-talk.

To implement these concepts effectively, begin with self-reflection. This process requires honesty, vulnerability, and introspection. Ask yourself what you want and need in a relationship and what you're willing to contribute. Be specific about your expectations and communicate them to your partner respectfully and assertively.

Remember that healthy relationships are built on mutual respect, trust, and open communication. Knowing your boundaries, standards, core values, and deal breakers forms the foundation for creating the fulfilling and meaningful relationships you deserve.

HEALING HEART MEDITATION

This meditation focuses on the practice of releasing someone from your heart and mind. This can be a difficult and painful process, but it is essential for your own growth and happiness.

1. Take a deep breath and allow yourself to relax, either sitting or lying down. Let your body sink into a comfortable position and let your mind settle into a calm state.

2. Take a moment to think about the person you want to release. This may be an ex-partner, a former friend, or anyone who has caused you pain and hurt. Allow yourself to feel the emotions that arise, but do not dwell on them. Instead, let them flow through you and release them with each breath.

3. Visualize a golden cord extending from your heart to the person you want to release. This cord represents the energetic connection that exists between you and the other person. See it clearly in your mind's eye and pay attention to any emotions or sensations that arise.

4. Now, imagine a bright white light flowing down from above and enveloping both you and the person you want to release. This light is warm and comforting, and it has the power to dissolve any negative attachments or emotions that may be holding you back.

5. As the light fills your body and surrounds you, see the golden cord begin to melt and dissolve. Watch as it fades away into the light, taking with it any lingering pain, hurt, or resentment that you may be holding on to.

6. As the cord disappears, imagine a feeling of lightness and freedom washing over you. You are no longer bound to this person by negative emotions or attachments. You are free to move forward with your life, unencumbered by the past.

7. As you finish your meditation, take a few deep breaths and allow yourself to return to the present moment.

Know that you have taken an important step toward healing and growth, and that you are capable of releasing anyone who no longer serves you.

8. Repeat this visualization as often as you need to. Remember that releasing someone is a process, and it may take time to fully let go. Be patient with yourself and trust that you will find the peace and happiness you deserve.

SIGNS THAT YOU'RE HEALING

When going through the aftermath of a difficult breakup, it's not uncommon to feel like you're wading through murky waters. Often, there's a haze of emotions, memories, and what-ifs that cloud your vision. It's like trying to navigate through a thick forest with no compass. However, healing is a journey, not a destination. It's an intricate process that unfolds layer by layer. What's essential to remember is that healing is not linear; there may be ups and downs, moments of doubt followed by moments of clarity. Now that you have truly begun to heal, it is time for you to turn your attention even deeper to your heart sabbatical. While every individual's healing process is unique, there are common signs that indicate progress on this journey.

- You no longer feel the need to constantly check your ex-partner's social media accounts. This shows that you are no longer seeking validation or trying to keep tabs on their life.

- You have learned to respect your own and other people's boundaries around communication.
- You understand that respecting their need for space is important for both of you to move on.
- You have become aware of patterns in your relationships, such as playing the savior, people-pleasing, auditioning, and performing. This means that you are making a conscious effort to not repeat these patterns, and you're able to build healthier relationships.
- You are discovering the beauty of solitude, finding joy and contentment in your own company, and embracing the moments you spend with yourself. This shows that you have developed a healthy relationship with yourself.
- Your desire to return to the cycle of uncertainty, confusion, and betrayal has diminished. You are no longer attracted to toxic or unhealthy relationships, and you are now able to recognize red flags and avoid them.
- You're compassionately reflecting on your past relationship, recognizing both your role in it and the areas where you weren't at fault. You're not only taking responsibility for your actions but also granting yourself grace for things outside of your control. This journey of understanding is accompanied by a deep sense of self-forgiveness, allowing you to embrace lessons without holding on to burdens.
- You are aware of your inner child's wounds and are

actively working to re-parent yourself. This means that you are addressing any unresolved childhood traumas and taking steps to heal from them.

- You now seek answers from your triggers instead of avoiding them. This means that you are willing to confront difficult emotions, rather than deflecting them through unhealthy coping mechanisms.

- You understand how your ego allowed you to chase unrequited love in order to avoid facing rejection. This means that you are no longer seeking validation from external sources and are instead building a strong sense of self-worth.

- Lastly, you have developed healthy boundaries and standards, and you know your core values. This shows that you have a clear idea of what you want and need in a relationship, and you are able to communicate those needs effectively.

Mara sat across from me, her eyes still puffy from crying. She had just received a call from her ex, who was trying to slip back into her life. But something had shifted in Mara since the last time they spoke.

He'd called while we were in session together. "I'm sorry, but I can't have any contact with you," she said firmly, drawing a line in the sand. This was the first time Mara had set a clear boundary with him, and she felt a sense of relief wash over her.

As we continued our session, Mara shared how she had been on a heart sabbatical, taking time to reflect and heal from the toxic relationship. Through this process, she had been learning about the importance of boundaries, standards, core values, and deal breakers in relationships. She realized that she had never really taken the time to define these for herself before.

Mara had always been a people-pleaser, saying yes to everything and everyone, even when it didn't align with her values or needs. But now, she was beginning to understand that boundaries were crucial to healthy relationships. She learned that a boundary was something she set to protect herself, like saying no to plans that didn't feel right or speaking up when someone crossed a line. She also realized that an ultimatum, like "if you don't do this, I'm leaving," wasn't a boundary but a form of control.

As we talked more, Mara began to redefine her standards for dating. She realized that she had settled for less than she deserved in the past, but knew now that she deserved someone who treated her with respect, kindness, and empathy. She also discovered new deal breakers, like someone who was emotionally unavailable or didn't prioritize their mental health. The reality is, a partner who doesn't, can't, or chooses not to prioritize their mental health is an emotional liability in a relationship. People who have inner conflicts yet refuse to go to therapy or work through their issues can end up being emotionally, verbally, and even physically abusive, evidenced by—and not limited to—covert aggression, manipulation, violent mood swings, and/or deception around extraneous sexual affairs.

Finally, Mara discovered her core values, the things that were most important to her in life. She realized that she had been living out of alignment for too long, but now she was committed to living a life that honored her values. These included honesty, integrity, and compassion.

Mara wished she had known about these concepts earlier in life, but I reminded her that it's never too late to learn and grow.

I am often asked, "When will I be ready to end my heart sabbatical?" My answer is: when your body feels it's time to do so. There's no predetermined time that's good for everyone. You'll likely take several heart sabbaticals over the course of your life for different reasons. Many of my clients prefer to remain on one for a longer period of time because they enjoy the process of reconnecting and giving themselves time to process the inner work.

My advice is to start with four months. As you move forward, focus less on the time period and more on the experiences. At the end of the four months, if you still feel that you need more time, continue on the sabbatical until you're ready to date again.

A heart sabbatical is like a retreat for your heart and soul. It's a time when you give yourself the love and attention you truly deserve, especially after dealing with a challenging or toxic relationship. One of the key things you do during this time is choose yourself over that toxic connection. It's a powerful act of self-love, and it's all about honoring your own emotional needs, even when someone else couldn't.

Now, it's tempting to point fingers at the other person for not meeting your emotional needs, but here's the real deal:

we can only control our own actions, including whether we abandon ourselves or stay true to who we are, no matter how tough it gets.

By choosing yourself over toxic relationships and taking steps to truly connect with yourself, you're laying the groundwork for healthier connections. Like nurturing a beautiful garden within your heart, this part of the healing journey paves the way for deeper emotional connections with yourself and those around you. In fact, choosing yourself is not just a part of the heart sabbatical—it's the core of it. It's where you begin to rediscover your inner compass, heal, and make meaningful connections in your life.

So, think of your heart sabbatical as a loving pause, a time to cherish yourself, and a path to building connections that truly nurture your soul. This is your journey, and it all starts with choosing yourself.

5

....

External Healing

I sat in my office with my client Gracie across from me. She took a deep breath, her gaze distant, lost in memories of a past that still haunted her. I leaned forward, my fingers steepled, watching her. I've always felt that the therapy room is sacred, a place where people can unravel their deepest fears and hopes. I had to tread gently. "Gracie," I began, my voice soft. "When we talk about your childhood and the things you saw, especially with your mom, how does that make you feel about your own choices?"

She blinked, fighting back tears, "I . . . I always thought it was normal, you know? Seeing Mom go through all that with Dad, and then the world outside whispering that women should be . . . I don't know, quieter? Submissive? It was like this heavy cloak I felt I had to wear."

I nodded, urging her to go on. "And when you think of how society views women, and the relationships you've seen around you, do you feel that influenced your choices with Jack?"

She took a moment, her fingers playing with the embroidered cushion beside her. "It's like everywhere I looked, I was being told a story. A story where women just took whatever was thrown at them. And I saw my mom wear that story like a badge. Maybe I thought that was my badge, too."

I paused, letting her words fill the space. "Gracie, society and culture do weave narratives for us. And sometimes, without realizing it, we start living those stories. Especially when they're mirrored in our homes. Do you think seeing your mom endure and accept what she did made you feel that it was your story to endure, too?"

She sighed, her eyes brimming with tears. "I guess, yes. Everywhere I turned, whether it was in movies, TV shows, or even just overheard conversations, the message was clear. If something went wrong, it was the woman's fault. And if she faced abuse, well, she probably did something to provoke it, right?"

I felt a pang of sadness. "Gracie, that's a heavy burden to carry. A script written by society, but not necessarily the truth for every individual. It's so essential to recognize these patterns and see how they might have influenced our choices, knowingly or unknowingly."

Gracie looked up, her voice quivering but determined. "I want to rewrite my story. I don't want the shadows of the past or society's flawed narrative to define me."

Smiling gently, I responded, "And that's why we're here, Gracie. To understand, to heal, and to chart a new path."

Gracie had been in a toxic relationship with her partner, Jack, for several years, and we'd been working together for four months. Gracie had experienced emotional abuse and manipulation in their relationship and felt trapped in the cycle of codependency. Despite recognizing that the relationship was toxic, Gracie had found it difficult to break free. I knew that much of it had to do with trauma bonding and manipulative behavior by her partner, but I felt there was something larger at play, as well: the societal norms and cultural expectations that often place the blame on the victim in these cases.

I'd been seeing a disturbing trend in my clients' stories that went beyond interpersonal dynamics. In today's dating culture, we have more awareness of terms like *gaslighting, manipulation,* and *narcissistic behavior.* But with this awareness I also see a tendency for society to blame women when they fall for all the lies and tricks that their partners pull. It's like this unspoken rule that somehow women are responsible for it all. But hold on, let's take a step back and think about it.

This kind of blame-shifting reflects a culture that all too often turns a blind eye to the manipulation, emotional unavailability, and, dare I say, sociopathic behavior that's out there. Instead of putting the blame on women who are looking for love and connection, we need to investigate where that blame really belongs. Yes, on the partner perpetuating the toxic behavior, but also on the society that does not condemn misogynistic behavior, instead facilitating systemic power dynamics that influence our interpersonal relationships. When it comes to toxic relationships, societal norms and cultural influences are just as important to examine as internal trauma. Gracie and Jack's relationship was just one example I've seen of how we keep these harmful and oppressive patterns alive, which do nothing but chip away at our self-worth and our power.

Let's dig into the societal messaging and conditioning that was influencing Gracie and Jack's relationship. On one hand,

Gracie may have been raised with cultural norms that perpetuated the idea that women should be submissive to men, leading
her to believe that the abuse she experiences is her own fault.
This, combined with witnessing her own mother being abused,
perpetuates Gracie's unconscious belief that normalizes abuse
in relationships.

On the other hand, Jack's relationship with his own mother
played a significant role in his behavior toward Gracie. Growing up with an emotionally distant mother left him feeling
"under-mothered." In an effort to assert control and address
this, Jack unconsciously created an abusive dynamic in the
relationship, trapping Gracie in a subservient and mothering
role. The imbalanced power dynamic created by societal, cultural, and psychological structures perpetuated emotional unavailability in both partners as repetitive compulsion ran their
emotional show.

We've discussed the role our own Pandora's box plays in our
relationship patterns, but how do cultural and societal pressures
influence us as well? Our relationships are shaped by the cultural, psychological/emotional, and societal structures around
us in ways that are both visible and invisible, and they can
lead to power dynamics within them. To fully heal and move
forward, we need to acknowledge the external as well as the
internal, and how they work together. We've already explored
internal healing, and will be going even deeper in Part 2, but in
this chapter we will investigate the external forces.

From an emotional and psychological perspective, Gracie may be experiencing unresolved trauma from witnessing
the abuse of her mother, which has perpetuated the belief

that abuse is normal in relationships. This can cause her to feel trapped in her relationship with Jack and unable to escape due to an existing trauma bond between them. In addition, Jack may have his own emotional and psychological issues that contribute to his abusive behavior, such as past trauma or feelings of inadequacy if he isn't able to dominate and control his partner.

The misogynistic cultural expectation that women should be submissive and obedient to their partners plays a significant role in Gracie's relationship with Jack. This cultural belief creates a power imbalance in their relationship, with Jack exerting control over Gracie and perpetuating the belief that the abuse is her fault. The idea that women should be submissive to men perpetuates the imbalance of power and parent-child dynamic we often find in abusive relationships. This does not apply to partners who have a relationship with a higher power, are emotionally healthy, and cultivate a partnership rather than a dictatorship with their partner.

Societal messaging and conditioning also contribute to the issues in Gracie's relationship. Gracie's mother was taught that a woman's place was in the home, and that she should be submissive to her husband, which perpetuates the belief that a woman's worth is tied to her husband and her ability to fulfill traditional gender roles. This societal messaging can also contribute to Gracie losing her sense of inherent power and the sovereignty to decide how she wants to show up in the world outside of her relationship. Jack may have normalized toxic and abusive behavior as a result of societal norms that perpetuate misogyny and oppression.

Gracie and Jack's relationship is the result of a complex interplay between emotional/psychological issues, misogynistic cultural beliefs, and societal messaging and conditioning. To break the cycle of toxic relationships and truly heal, Gracie and Jack must both work to address both the internal and external issues impacting their relationship.

In this chapter, I'll be discussing how external healing work is just as important as internal healing. Many toxic relationship dynamics are symptomatic of larger societal issues around toxic relationships and the perpetuation of misogyny and oppression. Healing and breaking the cycle of toxic relationships requires a collective effort to challenge and unlearn these harmful societal norms and beliefs.

With awareness of these sociocultural patterns and their role in perpetuating relationship trauma and toxic patterns, we can empower ourselves to create more equitable partnerships built on mutual respect and understanding. This is why healing must be a collective effort, one that requires us to actively challenge and dismantle the structures that perpetuate toxic relationships. Let's break it down.

CULTURAL STRUCTURES

Culture shapes our beliefs, values, and expectations. It influences what we think a relationship should look like, the qualities we seek in a partner, our understanding of gender roles and power dynamics, and how society perceives the success or failure of a relationship. Culture can also promote imbalanced power dynamics based on gender, where one partner holds power and influence over the other. Cultural messages can contribute to toxic relationships and encourage abusive behaviors.

SOCIETAL STRUCTURES

Societal structures can perpetuate toxic relationships by normalizing abusive behaviors and discouraging people from seeking help. For example, the stigma attached to mental health issues or victimhood can make people feel ashamed or even powerless to change their situation. Society also reinforces gender roles, which can lead to imbalanced power dynamics and discourage individuals from speaking up about abuse. Financial dependence can also make it difficult for someone to leave an unhealthy relationship. The societal structures that reinforce toxic dynamics must be acknowledged and changed in order to promote healthier relationships.

Toxic relationships don't just reflect individual problems; they reveal larger societal issues that stem from our cultural, psychological, and societal structures. We need to both acknowledge and work toward changing these if we want healthier relationships moving forward. Only then will we be able to create more nurturing connections with others based on mutual respect and understanding, without fear of judgment or abuse from those closest to us. Through awareness of ourselves and our environment, we can learn how to truly heal, breaking the cycle of toxic relationships and fostering healthier, more fulfilling connections with one another.

UNLEARNING MISOGYNY IN THE DATING WORLD AND EMBRACING CONSCIOUS LOVE

Before we delve into the intricacies of unlearning misogyny in the dating world, it's crucial to clarify that while our examples and discussions may predominantly refer to heterosexual relationships, the issues of toxic dynamics, misogyny, and the need for conscious love are universal. They can arise in any type of romantic relationship, regardless of the genders or orientations of the people involved. I believe in the importance of love that transcends all boundaries, and our goal is to foster healthy, respectful relationships across the spectrum.

As you embark on the journey of healing from relational trauma, it is important to acknowledge that the work is not limited to your individual experiences. Sociocultural beliefs and structures play a significant role in perpetuating toxic relationship dynamics, particularly those rooted in misogyny and patriarchal values.

It is imperative that we unlearn these beliefs and restructure the culture around dating and relationships to one that promotes equality, respect, and healthy communication. In doing so, we not only heal ourselves but also contribute to a larger societal shift toward a healthier and more compassionate understanding of love and partnership.

We all deserve to live a life filled with ease, free from the struggles of survival-based and toxic relationships. But unfortunately, the ongoing battle around femininity and masculinity has the dating pool locked in a chokehold. This pushes us into the trap of criticizing each other and ourselves, perpetuated by the patriarchal standards that dictate how women and men should present themselves to be loved and accepted.

Patriarchal societies have long imposed strict gender roles on men and women, expecting men to embody aggressive and dominant traits, while women are pressured to embody passive and submissive traits. These gender roles are not based on biology, but rather on cultural constructions that justify women's oppression and the repression of emotions in men.

Society tells men their value comes from how many women they have sex with or are able to control, as well as the money they make. Society tells women their value is attached to how attractive and vulnerable they make themselves to men. Why vulnerable? This trait is perceived to be desirable because it means women can be easily controlled and thus considered feminine.

In dating, these expectations put pressure on women to conform to *traditional* notions of how women should show up in order to attract men. This often involves displaying subservient traits and hiding "masculine" qualities, which is in many ways fueled by the conflation between feminine energy and patriarchal expectations of women.

Internalized misogyny refers to the way women internalize and display societal messages that diminish our power and worth. This can show up in various forms, including our behavior in relationships and in the dating world. Internalized misogyny leads women to believe that they must sacrifice their own desires and goals to fit into these gender roles. And if we are being completely honest, the self-esteem, self-concept, and self-worth of all involved are grounded in what one expects of the other.

However, there is a growing movement to challenge these harmful societal messages and create a more conscious dating culture. This requires self-reflection and the courage to confront and dismantle internalized beliefs and behaviors about gender. It also involves examining the intersections of our identities, including race, class, and ability, and how they impact our relationships and gendered expectations.

By taking a holistic approach to healing, we can cultivate a more conscious dating culture based on mutual respect, emotional growth, and communication, rather than one where power dynamics based on gender roles define what partnerships should look like.

Let's take a look at a few issues we will need to unlearn in order to create healthy partnerships grounded in conscious love and relating.

Focusing Solely on "What Men Want"

When it comes to navigating dating, career and entrepreneurial women can often face misogyny, being deemed "masculine" or "unattractive." This way of thinking is both narrow-minded and harmful, and it ignores how the dating landscape has changed. Women today are searching for partners who are likable, intelligent, and mature, and who know how to create safe spaces for them. As such, isn't it time we stopped prioritizing what men want in a relationship and started focusing on the emotional health, development, and safety of both parties?

Society often tells us that if we're not pleasing men, we're not good enough. But what about the man's role in being a healthy partner? It's time we shifted the focus away from women changing and conforming, and instead encouraged both people to do the inner work to become better partners. This will help us to cultivate deeper relationships and connections, and shift the focus from performative love to conscious love.

Though there may be some problematic messaging out there, thankfully we're in a time of transition. There's more dialogue than ever on why we need to ditch the "what men want" mentality and focus on what really matters in a relationship. Recognizing and valuing the spectrum of human experience and expression will also help us to work toward creating a more inclusive and equitable society for all.

Making Everything About Feminine vs. Masculine Energy

This short-sighted approach can damage not only our relationships, but also our worldview. We don't need to define everything in terms of feminine or masculine energy. We tell men that if they don't behave like an "alpha," they are weak and "feminine"—and then we wonder why some men resent the feminine yet crave its acceptance. We tell women who are financially independent and successful in their careers that they are "too masculine."

When we define individuals in this limited way, we fail to acknowledge the variety of human experience and expression. We need to work together to challenge and dismantle the harmful societal messages that have been imposed on us. In doing so, we will create a more compassionate and equitable world for all.

Equating Hyper-Independence with Masculine Energy

As women, we are often taught to be nurturing and receptive, but when we encounter someone who is "not open to receiving," it is important that we don't equate this with a lack of "femininity." Resistance to receiving help and support is often rooted in trauma, whether from cultural conditioning, difficult life experiences, or past betrayals and abandonment—and it affects both men and women.

When we teach men to avoid vulnerability, suppress their emotions, and reject help, we rob them of the chance to heal from and process their traumatic experiences. This double standard has serious consequences and contributes to the male mental health crisis. Internalized emotional suppression can manifest as anxiety, depression, anger, and addiction, and it can cause men to struggle with intimacy and connection in their relationships.

They may have trouble expressing themselves, sharing their feelings, and being truly present with their partners, which can lead to a breakdown of trust and communication (one of the primary reasons why relationships fail). Telling men to avoid vulnerability, while encouraging women to be open and receptive, creates a vicious cycle of emotional unavailability that damages relationships, perpetuates trauma, and undermines the mental and emotional well-being of everyone involved.

It's time to challenge these harmful gender norms and strive for a healthier and more balanced approach to relationships and mental health. We need to shift our perspective and acknowledge that this common trauma response impacts all of us. Let us embrace a more holistic and empathetic approach that recognizes and addresses the underlying traumas, rather than simply labeling and judging. By doing so, we can work toward creating a society that is more compassionate and equitable, one that supports healing and growth for all.

Defining Femininity Outside of Pleasing Men

Too often, we equate "feminine energy" with patriarchal notions of how women are expected to behave to please men. When we do this, it leads to harmful and limiting beliefs about femininity and what it means to be a woman. It's vital to recognize that we are culturally groomed to believe that certain appearances and behaviors are attractive. Rather than being rooted in biology, these stem from social and cultural expectations. "Feminine energy" is not a mask that we put on in order to get something—it's not about what we wear, how we present ourselves, or the way we behave. It is an energy that we embody as women, one that we can express in a myriad of ways.

It's time we rejected the limiting and harmful notion that there is only one way for women to be "feminine." Let's work toward creating a more inclusive and equitable society, one that supports and celebrates the diverse expressions of femininity in all their glory.

Promoting Imbalanced Power Dynamics

The notion of femininity has long been tangled with societal expectations and impositions. Historically, certain societal structures and norms often boxed women into specific roles, primarily based on the assumption that certain roles were "fit" for women and others weren't.

For instance, in many societies and cultures, women were encouraged or even compelled to embrace the role of homemaker, not necessarily because it was inherently a feminine role, but because societal norms and restrictions limited women's opportunities outside the home. These impositions weren't just about job roles; they were deeply intertwined with what was considered appropriate, respectable, and "feminine."

In communities or geographical regions where traditional values heavily influence societal norms, these attitudes persist. They may also linger in our personal and psychic structures. If, for example, our mothers or grandmothers held the belief that a woman's place was in the home, those thoughts might still unconsciously influence our perceptions.

Today, we're in a transformative era. Women across the world, especially in urban settings and dual-career households, have a broader array of choices available to them. However, in some regions or communities, particularly where cultural and traditional beliefs hold significant sway, remnants of these older perspectives about femininity persist. This isn't to say that choosing to be a homemaker is in any way inferior; it's the lack of choice or the imposition of a singular choice that's problematic.

Ultimately, the true essence of femininity is diverse, fluid, and deeply personal. It's vital that we recognize and celebrate this diversity, ensuring that every woman has the autonomy to define and express her femininity in a way that resonates with her individual identity, unshackled from outdated societal norms.

It is important to critically examine the trends and messaging that are often presented as "truth" about femininity and how women should show up in the world. Too often, these modern trends are based on outdated and harmful patriarchal notions that do nothing but reinforce toxic gender roles and internalized misogyny.

Let's stop regurgitating archaic patriarchal notions that we encounter on YouTube and other media platforms. Instead, let's take the time to critically examine the layers and nuances of these ideas and their impact on our lives and relationships. By doing so, we can work toward creating a more compassionate and equitable society for all.

DECODING THE SUBTEXT OF THE SEXIST MESSAGING IN DATING AND RELATIONSHIPS

The harmful messaging around women, their careers and finances, and imbalanced power dynamics is often disguised as advice. "Men don't care about your money or your degrees" is code for, "We want women to be hungry and destitute in order to keep them powerless and without options." It also promotes the idea that a woman's value only lies in what's attractive to her partner—not who she really is.

Amid this chatter, it's challenging to distinguish genuine discourse about relationships from old-fashioned societal expectations masquerading as "harmless" dating advice.

The Myth of Choosing Better

Have you ever heard someone say that if women just chose better, they wouldn't be in the situation they are in? Logically, this is true. However, the messengers are typically emotional predators who set out to "trick" their partners (using deception and manipulation) into getting what they want, later blaming them for falling for it. This is not only wrong, it's also a harmful narrative. We should stop telling women to choose better and instead focus on healing so that we can *all* be better without playing the blame game.

When we tell women to "choose better," we are perpetuating a narrative of victim-blaming while ignoring the other side; it takes all parties involved to produce the outcome. This dialogue implies that if a woman were just smarter or more aware, she would have made different choices and avoided whatever situation she found herself in—and it conveniently ignores how we as a society have condoned and even normalized toxic, harmful, and dysfunctional behavior.

We all need to choose better and we all need to do

better—we need to emphasize healing and growth for everyone. We need to cultivate self-reflection, empathy, and resilience in order to create healthier relationships with one another as well as within ourselves. We need to prioritize creating safe spaces where we can learn from our mistakes and grow from them, rather than being shamed for our past actions.

We must also recognize how societal norms contribute to this problem. For centuries, men have been taught that it is their right (or even duty) to control, dominate, and in some cultures, abuse women. At the same time, women have been socialized into believing that it is their responsibility to obey men, no matter what. We must dismantle these ideas if we want true gender equality and freedom from oppression.

Blaming victims only serves to reinforce oppressive systems of power and control over marginalized people—particularly women. Instead of victim-blaming, we should focus on creating environments where healing can take place through open dialogue, education, and understanding between genders, so that we can all be better together without relying on shame or guilt as motivators for change. Only then will we begin to see real progress toward a more balanced healing path.

The Myth of Male Disinterest in Female Success

One of the most pervasive messages surrounding courtship is that men don't care about female success or financial stability. This message is insidious because it reinforces the notion that independent women are undesirable, and it implies that the only way for a woman to attract male attention is to appear vulnerable or desperate. But this isn't true; healthy masculinity appreciates a woman's success just as much as it appreciates traditional femininity.

The Myth: Success Makes Women Less Desirable—Tales of Projection and Insecurity

The idea that men are inherently insecure or fragile when it comes to female success is rooted in a long-held belief that men need to be dominant and powerful. Unfortunately, this belief is perpetuated by our culture, which continues to depict women as less capable than men. This contributes to a sense of male insecurity around female success because they perceive it as a threat. In men, this can manifest itself as a fear of being "undermined" by successful women, which leads to feelings of insecurity and ego fragility.

For some men, the idea of having an equal partner who requires more than just money or sex can be difficult to cope with. In order for relationships between men and women to truly reach a state of equality, men must be willing to show up with emotional intelligence, depth, and maturity—qualities that may be lacking due to socialization around male dominance and misogynistic messaging that begins in childhood.

Socialization Around Male Dominance

Many boys are taught that they should strive for dominance over their female counterparts, a belief that often carries into adulthood. This mindset is grounded in antiquated ideals like the need for women to abdicate the inherent power granted by increased education and financial independence. If women are no longer opting to stay in relationships where they have less power than their partners, this goes against the patriarchal dynamic that requires them to abdicate their power in order to be seen as attractive.

The False Narrative of Femininity and Submission

Have you ever noticed that the idea of femininity is often equated with submissiveness? It's an insidious assumption that keeps getting perpetuated in our culture, from the movies we watch to the music we listen to. This false narrative has led to an unbalanced power dynamic between men and women, in which the man has all the power and the woman is expected to be a doormat. In reality, women can assert their femininity without having to submit themselves to men.

Let's talk about why these notions of femininity and submission are so harmful.

The Myth of Submissive Femininity

Conflating femininity with submission sends a message that women should be pleasing, passive, and accommodating in order for men to find them attractive. This message gets internalized by many women—and some men—and it leads to a skewed understanding of healthy relating. They think that in order for a relationship to work, one partner must always be submissive, which means one partner will always have more power than the other.

This goes against what true partnership should look like: a balanced exchange where both partners are on equal footing and recognize each other's needs. When there are unequal power dynamics present in a relationship, it creates an unhealthy environment where one partner feels entitled or superior. That kind of imbalance can lead to manipulation or even abuse—all because people have been conditioned into believing that submission is synonymous with being feminine.

The Need for True Partnership

True partnership requires a healthy exchange between two equals who respect each other's boundaries, needs, and wants, while also recognizing each other's strengths and weaknesses. This is one reason why diverse representation of women matters, particularly in the media. By seeing more strong female protagonists—women who are assertive, independent, and empowered without sacrificing their femininity or themselves at the altar of male dominance—we can start changing the false narrative around femininity once and for all!

True partnership cannot exist when there is an unbalanced power dynamic at play; a relationship in which one person holds all the cards while another person just plays along as if they don't matter. Yet, the idea that women must be submissive in order for them to hold any form of appeal or value toward men still persists, as does the belief that without submission, women won't progress in their personal or professional lives.

This could not be further from the truth.

Women can embrace their feminine side without having to sacrifice their autonomy or self-respect in doing so; they can remain strong and independent while still being seen as beautiful and desirable partners by men who understand that true partnership exists when both sides are on equal footing with love, instead of being led by fear. Women deserve partners who can see, hear, and honor their emotional needs.

Having an emotionally intelligent partner is essential for sustaining a long-term relationship filled with trust and understanding. Not only does emotional intelligence allow both partners to understand one another's feelings better, but it also encourages healthy dynamics between them by emphasizing mutual respect and support over contention or resentment. Ultimately, this type of partnership benefits both parties equally by creating strong connections that last through thick and thin.

Understanding Emotional Needs

It's important to find a partner who not only understands how you feel but can recognize when you are experiencing certain feelings. This requires an emotionally intelligent partner who has the ability to empathize with your perspective and recognize what you need in order to feel heard, respected, and safe. This type of partnership creates a sense of safety and security that helps foster trust and intimacy between the two of you.

Prioritizing Healthy Relationships

Having an emotionally intelligent partner means being with someone who prioritizes healthy relationships. This means that they will not only be aware of their own feelings but will also be conscious about how their behavior affects yours, and how it impacts the dynamic between the two of you. Instead of reacting impulsively or avoiding responsibility for their actions, an emotionally intelligent partner will take ownership over their behavior and strive to make amends if necessary.

A healthy relationship is one where both parties have equal footing—one where each person's individual needs are respected so that both can get what they need from the relationship without sacrificing too much on either side. By prioritizing healthy relationships, partners are able to create strong connections filled with mutual support and respect rather than contention or resentment. These types of partnerships tend to stand the test of time, because at their core is genuine care for one another.

What Needs to Change?

What we are seeing here is a deep-seated fear on the part of some men—and women—of engaging in balanced partnerships where both parties feel supported and seen for who they are without judgment or criticism. For some, this wasn't modeled in their homes growing up, and as such, they have no experience with it as adults.

This fear is often shrouded by cultural expectations around

gender roles that lead women, especially those struggling with codependency issues, to believe that their value and worth lies solely in pleasing men who have no desire to see them as equals deserving of holistic love and respect. However, when we understand why these fears exist, then we can begin to address them so that everyone involved can benefit from healthier relationships built on mutual understanding and respect rather than control and manipulation.

The Need for Control

At its core, this fear of an equal partnership is rooted in the need for control. Men who are afraid of being vulnerable often feel as though they need to be in control of the relationship and their partner's actions in order to feel safe. This can manifest in different ways, such as controlling behavior, manipulation, or emotional abuse. It can also look like an unwillingness to engage with their partner's feelings or concerns, and an overall lack of empathy.

The Fear of Vulnerability

Behind these behaviors lies a deeper fear—the fear of vulnerability. When someone has been hurt before, either during childhood or in past relationships, they may be scared to open themselves up and risk being hurt again. They may also be afraid that if they let go of the control they have over their relationships, something bad will happen and they won't be able to protect themselves or their partner from harm. As a result, they cling to power and control as a way of protecting themselves from potential pain.

If we want to meaningfully change the culture of male disinterest in female success, then we need both genders to work together toward greater understanding and empathy. Men must recognize their own biases while also learning how they can better support their partners' successes instead of viewing them as threats. Similarly, women must learn how to communicate effectively with their partners so that those conversations don't become confrontational or hostile. With both sides putting forth effort toward understanding one another more deeply, we can move closer toward creating relationships based on true equality.

Codependency Issues and Low Self-Esteem

Cultural gender dynamics can be especially damaging when there are also codependency issues at play. In codependent relationships, one person may define their worth and value through another person—namely their partner. When gender expectations are added to this mix, we can end up defining our worth based on someone who has no interest in seeing us holistically as an equal emotional partner. This dynamic leads to feelings of low self-worth and low self-esteem, creating an even greater sense of insecurity that can lead us back into patterns of imbalanced power dynamics out of necessity rather than choice.

Ultimately, what needs to change in these codependent relationships isn't just male insecurity around female success—it's also the unwillingness to accept an equal relationship where both parties bring something other than money or sex to the equation. By recognizing our own biases while also seeking out ways we can better support each other's successes, we can create healthier relationships based on mutual respect and understanding between both genders. It's time for us all—men included—to step up and make sure no one feels left behind in our pursuit of true equality within our society today!

The Power of Financial Independence

Financial independence is a key factor for many successful relationships because it helps couples maintain trust and equality within their relationship dynamics. When both partners have access to their own resources, couples tend to feel more secure in their relationship and empowered to make decisions without fear or pressure from their partner. It also makes it easier for couples to share responsibilities without feeling burdened by one partner's financial obligations over another's; when both people have financial independence, they can work together as equal partners toward common goals instead of competing against each other for resources.

The Reality Behind "Traditional" Gender Roles

At its core, the myth of male disinterest in female success is just another way for society to keep women in traditional gender roles—roles that allow men to maintain control over their relationships while keeping women powerless and without options.

In actuality, these kinds of gender roles are outdated and do not reflect the reality between modern couples; successful relationships are formed when either partner is free to pursue their own interests while also supporting the other's goals.

Women should never feel like they need to sacrifice their career aspirations or financial independence in order to find love or attraction from potential partners; rather than believing the myth that men don't care about female success, recognize it for what it truly is—a tool to keep women dependent on men so they won't have any power or options outside of traditional gender roles. By understanding how this myth works and refusing to subscribe to its message, we can challenge outdated beliefs around gender roles and help create space for healthier relationships between genders going forward.

FREEING OURSELVES FROM THE TRAP OF "THE ONE"

We all have this dream of finding that special someone who will love and support us, and make our lives complete. But here's the thing: life is so much more than just searching for "the one." It's about having a circle of healthy and loving relationships that bring joy and meaning to our lives. The most important thing we can do for ourselves is to love ourselves, embrace our worth, and be content in our own skin.

By doing this, we open ourselves up to finding true love and authentic connections—while also learning to be happy with ourselves outside of them.

As you learn how to thrive, you'll let go of any expectations you have about finding the one and focus on becoming the best version of yourself.

Codependency can put us in a trap of believing that we need to find the one, a soulmate, or a perfect partner to make us feel complete and happy. This can lead to unhealthy relationships with people who don't have our best interests in mind. To free ourselves from this trap and have healthier relationships, we must first accept that we are enough and shift our focus away from finding the one.

Why Do We Seek "The One"?

When we are trapped in the cycle of codependency, it is easy to get stuck on the idea that our happiness depends on finding a romantic soulmate or the one who will complete us. We start feeling like if we just find this perfect person who meets all our expectations and desires, then everything else will fall into place. We become so focused on this idealized version of love that we forget about ourselves and our own needs in the process. It can be hard to break out of this mindset because it feels safe—it gives us something tangible to strive for—but ultimately, it keeps us stuck in unhealthy patterns.

How Can We Shift Away from Focusing on "The One"?

In order to heal from codependency and create healthier relationships for ourselves, we must begin by shifting our focus away from finding the one or searching for external validation from another person. Instead, we must work toward accepting ourselves as worthy; we are deserving of love without having to search outside ourselves for it. This can involve engaging in self-care activities such as journaling, meditating, being mindful about how we speak to ourselves internally, or seeking help from a professional therapist if needed. Learning how to set healthy boundaries with others is also essential for creating thriving relationships because it helps us establish clear expectations within our interactions with others while still allowing space for self-expression outside the context of those relationships.

THE PERFECT PARTNER DOES NOT EXIST

We all want to find the perfect partner in life, don't we? Someone who understands us, loves us unconditionally, and appreciates our quirks. But what if I told you that this perfect person does not exist? It may be an unpopular opinion, but it's true.

Before you become discouraged, however, let me explain why this isn't necessarily a bad thing.

We often focus on looking for red flags when it comes to dating instead of seeking out green flags. Looking for red flags is important; it keeps us safe and helps us avoid unhealthy relationships. However, instead of just searching for red flags in order to protect ourselves from potential hurt or manipulation, why not focus on embodying the green flags? Instead of simply searching for a "perfect partner," why not strive to become one?

When it comes to a relationship with a soulmate or even

just someone we enjoy spending time with, both parties are constantly learning how to love each other better, growing together as they go through life. This means that the relationship will ebb and flow like the ocean tide—sometimes turbulent and other times calm, but never stagnant. Embrace these changes, because they make your relationship unique and meaningful.

No two people are ever exactly alike; there will always be differences between partners no matter how great their connection is or how compatible they appear to be on paper. This doesn't mean that you have chosen incorrectly; it means you chose wisely because you know what works for you better than anyone else does! Celebrate those differences because they are what makes each individual special. They add more depth and richness to your relationship as a whole.

The perfect partner does not exist, but that doesn't mean we should stop searching for something better than what we've been putting up with. Instead of looking for red flags in others so that you don't have to pay attention to your own, strive toward embodying green flags and cultivating a healthy partnership with someone who loves you unconditionally despite your imperfections. When two people are willing to learn from each other and grow together, anything is possible. Don't give up hope—keep looking until you find someone who brings out the best in you!

When navigating the dating world, it's important to be mindful of the advice you listen to. Unfortunately, some dating advice is rooted in codependency and insecure attachment, and it only leads to unfulfilling relationships and a lack of personal growth.

Here are some examples of unproductive dating advice to watch out for:

Playing Hard to Get: This approach may seem like a way to make someone interested in you, but it only creates a false sense of mystery and distance. In reality, it's better to be honest and genuine in your interactions.

Waiting for the Other Person to Make the First Move: This pattern reinforces the belief that you are not worthy, and it encourages a fear of rejection.

Not Being Too Eager: This advice suggests that showing too much interest is unattractive and will push someone away. In reality, being open and authentic about your feelings is a key aspect of a healthy relationship.

Rejecting Someone's Advances to Make Them Chase You: This is a manipulative and unhealthy approach to dating that can result in creating trauma bonds early in the relationship.

Not Asking About Someone's Intentions for Fear You'll Chase Them Away: This advice is based on the belief that being direct and asking for what you want is unattractive. However, having open and honest communication is the foundation of a healthy relationship.

Going with the Flow and Not Asking Questions: This approach encourages you to ignore your own needs and desires and go along with what someone else wants. It's important to be assertive and communicate your own wants and needs in a relationship. Next time you come across this type of unproductive dating advice, remember to prioritize your own needs and desires, be genuine and authentic in your interactions, and establish open and honest communication.

Part II

UNLOCKING THE PATTERN

PART II

UNLOCKING THE PATTERN

6

....

Shadow and Ego Work

My dad passed away when I was eleven years old. The last thing he said to me was, "Daddy will always be there for you." I still remember our last hug and watching him wave goodbye at the airport. He died three weeks later.

Years later, my therapist helped me appreciate that in the months after he passed, I was in denial. His death had been sudden and unexpected, and as a child I had a hard time believing he was gone. I didn't go to the funeral, so I had nothing to hold on to as closure. My therapist explained that I was still that little girl waiting for her dad to reappear. She helped me see how that trauma showed up in my life, even during something as trivial as a date. It was heavy.

Ah, there you are, repetitive compulsion. My therapist showed me how I was reenacting the pain of losing my dad and wondering whether he would ever come back home. I wanted the man I was dating to show up in the way that my dad didn't. My dad couldn't all those years ago, and whichever man I was dating at the time reenacted that. While I didn't consciously understand my father's unexpected death as abandonment, my inner little girl felt it that way and my ego was determined to create a different ending to the story. With every new man,

I gave my inner little girl hope that my dad—played by this person—would show up.

The highs and lows I experienced after my father's passing were also present in my dating life. I dated men who would bait me, ghost me, and then love-bomb me. The cycle mimicked the coupling of my childhood grief with my fantasy that my dad could soon return from a long trip.

My therapist said, "It was never about him," the man I was dating at the time. "This is about your dad."

That's when I met my attachment wounds and trauma responses, live and in color. I fawned amid this new man's empty apologies, holding back my own anxiety, sadness, and rage about how I was being treated—and, if I am honest, how I was allowing myself to be treated. I was paralyzed, waiting in the same way I waited for my dad to come through the door in the weeks and months after his death.

In this cycle, my inner child would spend days mourning the relationship with my dad all over again . . . and again . . . and again . . . and again. The trauma of losing him was deep. My heart had to break open so that my unconscious mind could understand what was actually happening. I chose and entertained this person because he mirrored my childhood patterns. His avoidance and eventual abandonment reminded me of the days and months leading up to my father's death, and while painful, it was familiar. I repeated the pattern over and over again, hoping for a different outcome that would never come.

These revelations forced me to take a deeper look at how I got here. My adult relationships didn't map onto my childhood experiences exactly, but there were commonalities that revealed greater truths about myself. To start with, I am the child of an affair. My father was still married to my sister's mother when he met my mother. One might expect that he wasn't around much, but it was quite the contrary. He was very present—we had a very close relationship. Yet lurking in the background was the knowledge that I was a secret. I also often worried I was unwanted by my mother. She was nineteen years old when she gave birth to me, and my arrival created deep rifts between her and her father. My father was two years younger than my grandfather and twenty years older than my mother.

Still, my father was a consistent emotional presence and financial provider to me and my mother even though he was still with his wife. But my mother would grow to resent his relationship with me.

He was there for me in ways her own father wasn't. My grandfather was intermittently absent from my mother's life due to his job as a cruise ship captain. So you can imagine what it feels like to watch your child get everything you desperately wanted from your own father. Her resentment of me ran deep, and I could feel it. My father acted as a buffer and my savior from her mood swings and tantrums, especially when they weren't getting along. But when he died, everything changed, and I was alone.

His death created deep abandonment and father wounds that I have fought long and hard to heal. Yet my conscious self was in denial of this. After all, he died unexpectedly and didn't leave me intentionally, right? However, his death meant I had to face the relationship with my mother head-on.

I lived with my father and aunts for a few years before his death because my mother was away at college. I would see her in the summer and on holidays, but otherwise I spent all my time with my dad. When he became ill, I moved to be with my mother, whom I hadn't lived with for a few years.

Suddenly, I was subject to her mood swings. I had to learn to fawn and people-please in order to sidestep her unpredictable wrath. It didn't matter if I was getting straight A's and doing all that a child is supposed to do in order to be "good" (hello, perfectionism). If her mood soured, anyone in the vicinity risked being a target. I'd go on to suffer verbal, physical, and emotional abuse as she too struggled with the loss of my father and the responsibility of having to parent me full-time. I was marinating in survival mode and struggling to manage complex traumas at just eleven years old. This is where my anxious attachment patterns became firmly established.

My story is far from unique. Many children experience these challenges growing up in one form or another; we even expect them to be resilient, because we were forced to be. Hello, intergenerational trauma! Older generations normalize their own trauma as a rite of passage, and describe it as something that makes you stronger. So, the children suffering in these situations experience their first taste of invalidation, which they then go on to normalize in their adult relationships.

Here we are, years later, running back to an emotionally unavailable ex who says our needs aren't valid and refuses to meet them. Their good looks aren't what keep you there. What keeps you there is a complex process where you're fighting a battle within yourself on multiple fronts: emotional, biological, and spiritual.

Let's take a deep breath together as we embark on this next chapter. You know, when I realized I had encoded my father's death as abandonment, it was like flipping on a light switch in a dark room. Going back into my history and connecting the dots with my current relationships was a roller coaster of emotions, but a necessary one. Sometimes our hearts carry unresolved trauma we're not even fully aware of, but it still shows up in how we relate to others and ourselves. In the following chapter, and across the entirety of Part 2, we'll be exploring this, starting with concepts like attachment, ego defenses, and how our past traumas might manifest in ways we don't immediately recognize, like my own tendencies to lean into denial and become a people-pleaser.

We covered a lot of ground in Part 1 and shed light on the difficult truths about toxic relationships. In the previous section, we started with how being in hermit mode and the heart sabbatical can help us begin to unpack our Pandora's box. But what happens once you've opened the box? Where does that leave us now? Well, you've done the first crucial part: you've recognized and healed from your past toxic relationship. It's like closing one chapter of a book. And as you turn the page, we're about to begin another equally, if not more, important chapter: the deep work.

Over the next few months, I'll be your guide as we trace back to the very roots of where these patterns originated. Think of it as a journey of self-discovery. It's not about pointing fingers or placing blame, but rather about understanding how we've been molded by our experiences. We're going to look back and understand why we react the way we do in relationships, whether they're platonic, professional, familial, or romantic.

This won't be a quick-fix process, and it's essential to manage our expectations. Real growth and understanding take time. With patience, introspection, and a genuine commitment to change, we can reshape our relational patterns and move toward a life filled with healthier and more fulfilling connections. So, as we step into this new chapter, I want you to remember one thing: you're not alone in this. Together, we'll unpack the complexities of our past to build a brighter, more authentic future. Join me as we navigate these intricate paths, understanding and healing as we go.

Embarking on the journey of addressing our ego and shadow aspects is a critical step in healing after relational trauma—or quite simply as a function of learning how to show up as an emotionally healthy human being. Whether it be with a romantic partner, family member, or friend, navigating relationships can leave us feeling drained and overwhelmed. With the right tools and approach, we can overcome these challenges and emerge stronger and more resilient. By delving into self-awareness and gaining a deeper understanding of our emotions, we develop greater emotional maturity and intelligence, ultimately learning how to build loving and safe connections with others. These skills are invaluable for navigating life after a toxic relationship and creating healthier relationships in the future. We're unlearning the past and building toward a more connected future with the people we love.

We went over ego and shadow work briefly in Part 1, but here we will delve deeper into both topics and look at the importance of these practices in the aftermath of a toxic relationship. Ego and shadow work are two components in the process of understanding the parts of ourselves that make up our personality, both conscious and unconscious. We all have an ego (conscious) side and a shadow (unconscious) side.

WHAT IS EGO WORK?

The ego consists of all the aspects of ourselves we are consciously aware of—our opinions, beliefs, and desires—while the shadow contains those aspects that are hidden from us—our fears, shame, and repressed emotions.

There are many ways the ego can show up in relationships. Some common examples include:

Need for Control: One partner may feel the need to control the relationship, making decisions for both partners and micromanaging every aspect of their lives together.

Defensiveness: The ego may make one partner become defensive when criticized or confronted, leading to arguments or a breakdown in communication.

Jealousy: Jealousy is a common manifestation of the ego in relationships, where one partner may feel threatened by the attention or affection given to the other.

Inflated Sense of Self: One partner may have an inflated sense of self, leading them to believe they are always right, or that their needs and opinions are more important than their partner's.

Rigidity: The ego may make one partner rigid in their beliefs and attitudes, leading them to resist change and growth in the relationship.

One of the most common ways I work with clients on the role their ego plays in their relationships is unpacking their defense mechanisms. Many of us have experienced codependent, traumatic, or toxic relationships at some point in our lives. While it's easy to blame the other person for the hurt we've endured, it's important to understand that our own defense mechanisms—the ways we protect ourselves from further harm—can play an equally important role in these relationships. Defense mechanisms are an active part of our ego, since they are conscious decisions we make. Let's explore how defense mechanisms show up in response to codependency, relational trauma, and toxic relationships.

What Are Defense Mechanisms?

Defense mechanisms are psychological tactics that our mind uses to cope with difficult emotions or situations. They can be either intentional or automatic, and can vary from healthy methods, like expressing one's feelings, to unhealthy ones, such as denying reality. Defense mechanisms serve two main purposes: they provide a barrier against potentially harmful or unpleasant experiences, and they allow us to process and understand our circumstances in a way that lessens ongoing fear or anxiety.

We utilize defense mechanisms in a number of different types of unhealthy relationship dynamics. In response to relational trauma, these mechanisms can provide a temporary sense of safety and stability, though they can also lead to longer-term problems if not addressed. In other codependent relationships, defense mechanisms are frequently employed to cope with the challenges and difficulties inherent to these types of connections.

While defense mechanisms can provide a sense of safety and control in the short term, they can also prevent us from processing and resolving relational trauma. It is important for those who have experienced relational trauma to seek support from a therapist or support group in order to address and heal from these experiences in a healthy and productive manner. By being aware of our defense mechanisms and their effects, we can work toward using more adaptive coping methods for better mental and emotional health.

In toxic relationships, one person might use tactics like gaslighting or emotional blackmailing to gain the upper hand. On the receiving end of these behaviors, it's common for us to lean on defense mechanisms. Recognizing these defense mechanisms is key because it can be the first step in understanding the dynamics at play and making the choice to seek a healthier path. The following are a few of the most common defense mechanisms used in toxic relationships, along with examples.

Splitting

Splitting is like looking at the world through glasses that only show two colors: all good or all bad. Sometimes, when people are still on their journey of understanding themselves and their emotions, they might see things this way. Imagine feeling so swamped by emotions that it's easier to categorize things as simply right or wrong, good or bad. It's like turning the volume up on a song—everything becomes more intense. That's when this black-and-white thinking sneaks in, leading to what we call "splitting." This allows a person to ignore any of their partner's flaws and only focus on the positive aspects of the relationship. In extreme cases, splitting can lead someone to stay in an abusive relationship because they refuse to accept that their partner has a dark side. Splitting makes it easier for a toxic partner to do whatever they want without consequences, as their victim continues to believe that things will improve if they just stay in the relationship long enough.

This defense mechanism is often used by people who are in emotionally volatile relationships. By mentally separating themselves from their partner's negative behaviors or words, they can better cope with the stress and uncertainty of the situation. In other words, they focus on the positive aspects of the relationship, ignoring or downplaying the more toxic side. This allows them to maintain some semblance of control over their lives and remain optimistic about their future, despite any turmoil they may be facing.

While psychological splitting can give someone a sense of security, it can also be damaging if it goes unchecked. By denying the negative aspects of their relationship, they are essentially enabling their partner's bad behavior and prolonging their suffering. Moreover, this type of thinking can lead someone into an unhealthy cycle where they constantly need reassurance from their partner that everything will be alright—only to discover that nothing has changed when they eventually receive that assurance.

It's important to recognize psychological splitting early on if you want to avoid becoming ensnared in a toxic relationship. Here are some signs that you may be experiencing psychological splitting:

- You find yourself feeling "all or nothing" about your partner—either loving them unconditionally or despising them with equal intensity.
- You feel constantly anxious when interacting with your partner.
- You are unable to engage in meaningful conversations without feeling overwhelmed.
- You have difficulty understanding why your partner does certain things.
- Your mood fluctuates wildly between positive and negative states without warning.

Idealizing

Idealizing is a defense mechanism that involves perceiving a toxic partner in an overly positive light. This can involve ignoring or downplaying negative behaviors, such as abuse or manipulation, and instead focusing on the perceived positive qualities of the partner. Idealizing can lead someone to view their partner as perfect or ideal, even in the face of evidence that suggests otherwise.

As a result, the person may remain in a toxic relationship, even when there are clear warning signs, because they have an unrealistic view of their partner and believe that everything is okay. This type of defense mechanism can be destructive, as it can prevent someone from recognizing and addressing the negative aspects of the relationship. It can also lead to a cycle of abuse and harm.

Here are a few examples of idealizing in toxic relationships:

- You believe that your partner's controlling behavior is a sign of love and care, even though it limits your freedom and autonomy.
- You ignore their partner's emotional abuse and instead focus on their positive qualities, such as their intelligence or sense of humor.
- You choose to overlook your partner's infidelity and instead focus on the good times you have together.

These examples illustrate how idealizing can lead a person to ignore the harmful aspects of a relationship and focus only on what they believe is good. It can prevent someone from recognizing the toxic nature of the relationship and taking steps to end it.

Denial

Denial is a defense mechanism that can be especially dangerous in toxic relationships. It involves refusing to accept the reality of a situation. Often, this can involve ignoring warning signs and negative experiences, instead clinging to the belief that everything is okay between you and your partner. For example, a codependent person may deny that their partner has a substance abuse problem. A victim of domestic abuse might deny that their partner is controlling or violent. Another example could be a person who is in a relationship with someone who is emotionally manipulative but refuses to acknowledge the manipulation. Despite evidence to the contrary, they may deny the reality, instead believing that their partner loves them and that things will get better in the future.

Denial provides a temporary escape from difficult emotions and the reality of a toxic relationship, but it can also lead to a dangerous cycle of abuse. It's important for those who find themselves in toxic relationships to confront their reality, seek help and support, and take steps toward a healthier and safer future.

Examples of denial in toxic relationships can include:

- Refusing to believe that your partner is abusive or manipulative, even when there is overwhelming evidence.
- Ignoring red flags and warning signs about your partner's behavior, such as controlling or possessive behavior, substance abuse, infidelity, or physical violence.
- Excusing your partner's harmful actions by blaming

yourself or other external factors, such as stress or
alcohol.

- Continuing to see your partner as a good person even
  when they repeatedly engage in harmful behaviors.
- Staying in a relationship despite feeling unsafe, unsupported, or unhappy, because you believe things will get
  better if you just try harder or love your partner more.

Denial is a powerful defense mechanism that allows people
to avoid confronting the reality of their toxic relationships, but
it also keeps them stuck in harmful cycles of abuse and reinforces negative patterns.

Here are brief overviews of additional defense mechanisms
I often see used by those in codependent or toxic relationships:

Repression: Pushing difficult emotions or experiences into
the unconscious mind in order to avoid dealing with
them. A codependent person may repress their feelings
of anger or frustration toward their partner's behavior.

Displacement: Redirecting feelings from one target to another. For example, a codependent person may displace
their anger toward their partner onto a coworker or
family member.

Projection: Attributing one's own thoughts, feelings, or
behaviors to others. A codependent person may project
their own insecurities onto their partner, accusing them
of being unfaithful or untrustworthy.

Passive Aggression: Indirectly expressing anger or frustration through passive means, such as sulking, procrasti-

nation, or neglect. A codependent person may express passive aggression toward their partner by not following through on promises or neglecting household chores.

Avoidance Behaviors: Avoiding confronting the reality of a situation. A codependent person may avoid addressing their partner's problematic behavior or substance abuse by ignoring it or changing the subject.

Dissociation: Detaching oneself emotionally from the situation or experience. This can take the form of feeling like an observer of one's own life, feeling disconnected from one's emotions, or feeling like time is moving in slow motion. Dissociation can provide a temporary escape from overwhelming emotions, but can also make it difficult to process and integrate the experience.

Compartmentalization: Separating different aspects of one's life into separate compartments in order to avoid confronting the trauma. For example, someone who has experienced relational trauma may compartmentalize their past experiences from their present-day relationships, instead focusing solely on the present.

Repressing Memories: Focusing on present-day needs rather than reflecting on past experiences. Repressing memories can provide a person temporary relief from the pain of the trauma, but it can also prevent them from processing and resolving the experience.

Numbing Oneself Emotionally: Avoiding feeling intense emotions by numbing oneself. This can involve using substances like alcohol or drugs, engaging in compulsive behaviors like overeating or gambling, or simply avoiding any situation that might trigger intense emotions. Numbing oneself emotionally can provide short-term relief, but can also lead to longer-term problems with addiction or compulsive behavior.

Ego work, or unpacking and understanding these conscious behaviors and patterns, has the potential to drastically improve your mental health following a period of codependency or toxic relationships. This work helps you become more aware of your own emotions while also allowing you to learn important lessons about setting healthy boundaries in all aspects of your life. It encourages you to explore your innermost thoughts without judgment, helping you heal from a toxic relationship as well as deeper trauma.

WHAT IS THE SHADOW?

The term "shadow" comes from Jungian psychology and is defined as the unconscious mind, or the repressed feelings and desires that we don't want to admit we have. Our shadows contain both positive and negative qualities, and they can manifest in various ways such as fear, anger, shame, guilt, or envy. We tend to deny these parts of ourselves out of shame or fear of judgment, but when they come out in relationships they can be damaging if not managed carefully.

We all have a "shadow" side, aspects of ourselves that contain qualities we don't want to admit. It's the part of us that holds our fears, insecurities, and unresolved wounds. In relationships, it can be easy to project this shadow onto our partners and make them responsible for what we are feeling. They become mirrors reflecting parts of our shadow we aren't aware of.

While it can feel intimidating to explore this part of ourselves head-on, it's important to understand that our shadow often shows up in our relationships with others. The truth is, our shadows are ours and no one else's. It's up to us to protect our partners from being cast in an unfavorable light by this part of ourselves. It's our responsibility, and honestly, our gift to them and to ourselves, to ensure we recognize and manage these reflections. In doing so, we're not just healing ourselves, but also cultivating healthier, more empathetic relationships.

Here are some examples of how our shadow plays out in relationships:

Insecurity and Jealousy

One of the most common ways our shadow manifests is through insecurity and jealousy. If we have unresolved issues from childhood or past relationships, we may carry these into our current ones and project them onto those closest to us. This can manifest as always questioning if the other person is being truthful or if they're going to leave us for someone better. It can also lead to feelings of jealousy when the other person spends time with or expresses interest in anyone else. This can cause unnecessary tension and hurt feelings within the relationship if not addressed properly, which we will discuss in more detail later on.

Fear and Control

Another way our shadow shows up is through fear and control. When faced with difficult emotions like fear, shame, or guilt, we may try to control our partner's behavior in order to protect ourselves from feeling vulnerable or overwhelmed by the situation at hand. This could include anything from trying to control their words and actions to constantly needing reassurance that they still care about us. While this behavior may temporarily make us feel better, it will almost always cause more damage in the long run as it chips away at trust and communication within the relationship.

Unresolved Trauma

Finally, unresolved trauma can also affect how we show up in relationships with others. If we suffer from PTSD due to past trauma, for example, we may find ourselves struggling with anxiety or depression when faced with certain triggers like disagreements within a relationship. We may also find ourselves engaging in destructive behaviors such as self-sabotage or manipulation as a way of protecting ourselves from getting hurt again by another person (or even by ourselves).

Because the shadow is unconscious, it can be tricky to spot in our relationships—and without recognizing our shadows, we can unwittingly cause tension. Imagine someone with deep feelings of jealousy. Their fear of loss might push them to check their partner's phone or feel a pang of anxiety at a simple conversation their partner has with someone else. They might not even realize the root of their actions, but this can put a strain on the relationship.

Let's consider a few more examples:

- Someone with shadowed anger might genuinely long for tranquility in their relationship, but find themselves occasionally snapping or slipping into heated disagreements.
- A person with hidden pockets of low self-worth might unknowingly lean on their partner for constant reassurance, not realizing the weight of their dependency.
- Someone guarding a past of deceit may occasionally hide truths, casting shadows of doubt over a bond that they truly value.
- Those with a concealed fear of intimacy might unknowingly maintain an emotional barrier, yearning to connect but unsure how.

In relationships with hints of codependency, these shadows can become even more pronounced. You might seek affirmation due to a concealed self-doubt, while your partner, battling their own shadows, might feel compelled to guide or even control the relationship. This dance, while unintentional, can often lead both parties down a path of emotional exhaustion with each other. And, in more painful scenarios, these shadows can even morph into actions that no one truly wants: verbal conflicts, emotional imbalances, or, tragically, physical confrontations.

But here's the silver lining: recognizing these shadows is the very first step to transformation. The first step in protecting your partner from your shadow is owning it. This means recognizing and responding to your own thoughts and feelings without projecting them onto others. The next step is understanding how these thoughts affect your behavior toward your partner: Do you become overly critical or defensive? Do you take out your stress on them? Awareness of how the shadow manifests itself will help you identify how you can shift the cycle in a healthier direction.

No relationship is perfect, but there are two crucial steps we can take to make sure our shadows don't fall too much on those we love most. First, owning our shadows requires the self-awareness to recognize when we're projecting our negative qualities onto our partners instead of dealing with them ourselves. Second, we must work to create a safe space for both parties to share their true feelings without fear or judgment. With these two pieces working together, couples can build more meaningful relationships where everyone involved feels respected and valued no matter what challenges arise along the way.

The most important factor in protecting your partner from your shadow is communication. Being open and honest with yourself and your partner can create a safe space where each person feels comfortable expressing their true feelings without fear of judgment or retaliation. It also allows you to work together toward identifying potential triggers for negative behavior before they occur and finding more productive ways to handle them should they happen again in the future. It may also be helpful to seek professional counseling if needed, so that you have someone guiding the process who is unbiased and experienced in navigating these kinds of issues within relationships.

Our shadow side can be difficult to confront, but understanding how it shows up in relationships is an important step toward healing and self-growth. By recognizing where these patterns come from, and why they emerged, we can begin working on managing them more effectively so that they no longer sabotage our relationships with others.

By embracing ego and shadow work, you're granting yourself the gift of self-awareness. You'll unearth those tucked-away feelings and, with compassion and understanding, reshape how you present yourself in your relationships. With mindful awareness and honest communication, you can move forward into healthier partnerships full of trust and mutual respect—because every relationship deserves a strong foundation.

THE BENEFITS OF DOING EGO AND SHADOW WORK

Embarking on the introspective journey of ego and shadow work is like being invited to read a diary we never knew we penned, confronting memories, emotions, and motives that have been woven silently into the very fabric of our beings. The introspection can be as delicate as threading a needle—we might fear pricking our finger, recalling moments of pain or self-doubt. Yet, as we'll see with my former client Sara, it's through this intimate self-reflection that we uncover the most profound truths about our relationships and ourselves. As we delve into Sara's story, we'll witness the transformative power of self-awareness.

As Sara settled into the chair across from me, I could see that she was struggling.

"Sara," I began gently, "tell me what's on your mind."

She took a deep breath, her fingers fidgeting in her lap. "I've worked tirelessly to escape the shadow of growing up in poverty. Today, I'm financially successful, but it feels like this very success is driving a wedge between Greg and me."

I nodded, understanding how she felt. "It sounds like your financial status, something you worked so hard for, is becoming a source of tension in your relationship."

"Yes," she whispered, tears forming in her eyes. "Sometimes I feel superior to Greg because of the money I make, and I resent him for not striving as hard. I hate admitting this, but it's the truth."

I leaned forward, hoping she would feel seen and heard. "It's brave of you to acknowledge that our backgrounds and past experiences often influence our present in ways we might not realize."

She looked up, her eyes searching for answers. "And what about Greg?"

Drawing from our previous sessions, I recounted, "Greg has grown up with the traditional belief that he should be the provider. Earning less than you challenges his deep-seated notions of masculinity and success. He might be manifesting his insecurities through passive-aggressive behaviors as a way to regain a sense of control."

Sara's face reflected the dawning realization. "So, we're both letting our egos and shadows sabotage our relationship?"

"In a way, yes," I replied. "For you to confront these responses, Sara, it would require introspection into how your past shapes your present sense of worth. And for Greg, he needs to challenge the societal expectations he has internalized."

She wiped away a tear, determination in her eyes. "We need to work on ourselves. At times it feels so hard, but it's necessary."

I smiled, feeling a spark of hope for Sara and Greg. "That's the spirit. Remember, this journey of self-awareness and growth, though challenging, will lead to a deeper connection and understanding."

Engaging in this type of inner exploration provides many benefits beyond just breaking free from toxic relationships. Doing ego and shadow work leads to increased emotional maturity; we can take responsibility for our actions once we recognize how our past experiences may have impacted us in ways we weren't aware of before. It also helps foster greater emotional intelligence by teaching us how to be mindful about our reactions when faced with difficult emotions. Additionally, engaging in this type of personal growth increases our self-awareness, which leads to improved decision-making and communication skills.

Engaging in ego and shadow work is essential when healing after a toxic relationship because it allows us to gain greater insight into why these unhealthy dynamics existed in the first place. It also helps us develop more effective coping skills for any future challenges that may arise. When done correctly, these exercises help build confidence while honing valuable qualities such as increased self-awareness, emotional depth, emotional maturity, and emotional intelligence—all necessary components needed when navigating life's ever-changing landscape.

Through healing, we shed parts of us that adapted to survival responses. Now, we learn to adapt to emotional peace that can help us heal and grow, leading to more authentic and fulfilling relationships with ourselves and others.

This work isn't easy, though, and psychological roadblocks often keep us from being able to engage with our ego and shadow. So, what might keep us from doing this important work? One of these major roadblocks is survival mode, which we'll discuss in the next chapter.

7
· · · · · · · · · ·

Survival Mode

Sometimes, it's hard to see the work that needs to be done. We may not even be aware that becoming the best version of ourselves is possible. I see this most in my clients who are experiencing chronic survival mode. In survival mode, they aren't able to live up to the full expanse of their potential because they're nursing wounds that limit emotional growth.

If you are wondering whether this is you, one clue is whether you've ever felt "normal" and safe in your own body. For people who have spent a large portion of their life in survival mode, there is often a pervasive struggle with battling triggers and attachment wounds. This can look like scanning the environment for threats (hypervigilance), avoiding situations that create threats, or the compulsion to entertain relationships that inflame threats. When you live in survival mode, your brain focuses on using significant events of the past to predict what lies ahead. Unbeknownst to you, your brain is constantly scanning your environment for familiar touchpoints in order to help you navigate life predictably.

Your brain has one job: to keep you alive. And if it is able to predict and navigate what's ahead while keeping you alive, then the job is done! But by doing this, we resist change. Adapting to change means accepting a period of time where the dynamic is unknown. This is especially true in your interpersonal relationships. In order to keep you alive after a traumatic event, your body must anticipate what's next. And believe it or not, this can mean choosing familiarity even when it is unsafe, since at least you know what to expect and how to navigate this dynamic. This is one way we fall into unhealthy patterns.

Here are a few examples of what our relationships can look like when we're living in survival mode:

Living in Extremes: Needing intense chemistry and emotional volatility. Cycling between make-ups and break-ups to feel loved in a relationship.

Obsession and Preoccupation: Obsessing about a new partner by fantasizing, romanticizing, idealizing, or love-bombing. Staying preoccupied by how a new partner feels about you while ignoring how you feel about them because you're focused on being chosen.

Emotional Volatility: Vacillating between love-bombing, breadcrumbing, and ghosting, creating intense emotional highs and lows. Initiating push-pull behavior when uncertain about a partner's intentions or when you need to maintain control.

Living on Autopilot: Being reactive, cycling between high anxiety and depression, and neglecting self-care and activities as your body does its best to cope while you're living in survival mode.

Avoidance: Walling yourself off from emotional connections because they feel too intense and overwhelming, or feeling afraid of showing vulnerability.

Disconnection: Distracting yourself with drugs, alcohol, emotionally addictive relationships, romanticizing, or fantasizing to avoid the pain after a breakup.

Insecurity and Low Self-Worth: Comparing yourself to your friends or your partner's exes, sometimes to the extent that you become obsessed with becoming a version of them or better than them.

Self-Abandonment and Self-Betrayal: Chronic people-pleasing to secure love, attention, and affection.

Notice the constant presence of emotional extremes. It's no wonder some might resort to relationships that make them feel good in the moment, only to have those relationships blaze like a forest fire and end just as quickly as they started. In many ways, these relationships burn out quickly because we're often chasing the high of new love to distract us from our pain.

THE UNCONSCIOUS MIND

At the heart of our choices, especially in relationships, is our unconscious mind. It's like an inner compass, shaped by early experiences, trying to guide us. It wants us to understand ourselves better, especially the patterns we may unknowingly repeat.

Growing up, your parents or caregivers sketched out the first draft of what relationships look like. As kids, our brains are like sponges, soaking up these lessons. For those of us who grew up always on alert, always in "survival mode," healthy relationships can feel unsettling. When you're used to chaos, calm waters can seem suspicious.

But recognizing these patterns is the magic key. It's like turning on a light in a dark room. The truth is, if our families didn't prioritize emotional safety when we were young, it's tricky for us to understand or offer it as adults. This is where cycles begin—each generation unintentionally passing on the same patterns. Unresolved trauma doesn't just haunt our minds; it affects our bodies, too. You might find yourself always tired, even if you're eating right and sleeping well. For some, this lingering trauma messes up sleep, leading to mood swings, anxiety, and sometimes depression. And to cope, many turn to the comfort of new relationships. A new relationship is like a spark in the dark—it's exciting and refreshing. All the old insecurities fade away when this new connection makes us feel valued.

But here's the catch: those old issues? They have a way of sneaking back. That realization hit me hard. After my divorce, the emotional weight of it all only truly sunk in a few months later. Looking back, I was constantly on edge, never truly feeling settled or safe anywhere.

Survival mode is isolating. It's like being trapped in a maze of our own making. We yearn for more but keep walking the same loops, influenced by the patterns we learned early on. It's like living on a tightrope—always tense, prioritizing others and neglecting ourselves.

This can look like:

- Being the resident fixer (attending to emergencies for everyone).
- Being hypercritical, argumentative, or crying easily; you're in a constant battle with yourself and others.
- Not engaging with play, creativity, or joy; rarely taking the time to decompress (not to be confused with numbing out); difficulty sleeping and always needing more down time.
- Rarely making future plans because the intensity of the present is too much.
- Denying and normalizing generational trauma because you're wedded to repeating patterns that allowed you to survive; resistance to being curious around these patterns.
- Feeling tired, stressed, and overwhelmed all the time; low sex drive.

The closeness of intimacy, the raw exposure of vulnerability, and the depth of genuine connections can sometimes feel like foreign territories for someone who has spent much of their life in survival mode. Why? Imagine growing up where chaos was the norm, where the unpredictable was predictable. These environments mold our perspectives, teaching us that true closeness means potential pain. We might unintentionally derail relationships when they come too close, or choose ones that stir up chaos and uncertainty. This isn't just being difficult; it's a defense mechanism. If we're always amid confusion, we never have to truly let our guard down and risk getting hurt in new ways. This can make it hard to dive in and do the work.

This internal script can play out in multiple ways:

Unfamiliar Territory: Intimacy and deep connections become foreign lands. Venturing there feels like setting foot in an unknown world, with threats lurking. This unfamiliarity can push you into the arms of relationships that echo the chaos and confusion of the past, just because it's what you know.

Self-Sabotage: Getting too close feels dangerous. So, consciously or unconsciously, you might push partners away before they can potentially hurt you. It's a protective mechanism, ensuring emotional safety even if it results in loneliness.

Fear of Abandonment: Ironically, the very fear of being left can drive behaviors ensuring it happens. You might gravitate toward partners who won't stay, or push them away through neglect or constant testing of their loyalty.

In relationships, these beliefs manifest in distinct patterns:

Surface Interactions: You keep things light and casual. Deep dives into feelings? They're avoided, which leads to emotional distance.

Mood Swings: You're in a constant swing between pessimism and optimism. Every situation, no matter how minor, feels like a looming crisis.

Anticipating Chaos: Even in peaceful moments, there's a nagging feeling that something will go wrong. It's like always waiting for the rain, even under clear skies.

Staying Busy to Create Avoidance: Overloading life with tasks and "busy work" provides a sense of purpose. But it's ultimately a distraction, a way to avoid confronting emotional pain.

Overthinking Control: Even if you think you're laid-back, there's a constant background noise of things you believe you should control.

With all these patterns, it's no wonder the body and mind feel out of sync. This is why you might feel like you're living in a constant state of high alert, even when there's no apparent threat. It's like being in perpetual survival mode, distanced from your true emotional and physical needs.

Adding to that, unresolved emotional trauma results in toxic shame. You believe there is something inherently wrong with you, so you search externally for something to fix and distract from yourself.

This is where toxic relationships and codependency feed into each other.

As much as you want to feel loved—you might even dream and fantasize about it—it's still foreign to you if you grew up with parents who were themselves in survival mode, leaving you feeling unwanted and unloved. Now, you might think,

Why would I want to repeat these patterns? Why would I want to get into a relationship that mirrors what I experienced growing up? This goes back to how our brains crave the familiar. Even if the familiar isn't healthy, it is still predictable. Your brain is actively resisting change.

This cycle perpetuates survival mode; you're living unconsciously on autopilot, choosing the same experiences because they're familiar to you. For example, if you grew up with a parent who was emotionally distant, you may choose a partner who is avoidantly attached and unable to meet your emotional needs around connection and closeness. Even if you desperately want to be loved and find the love you've always wanted, there's a part of you that might still feel unworthy and unlovable, so you engage in behavior that sabotages the relationship.

This is your body's way of protecting you from further harm, but it can also keep you trapped in survival mode, choosing familiarity over emotional health in a process called repetitive compulsion.

REPETITIVE COMPULSION

Think of repetitive compulsion like a playlist on repeat. Even though we might have hundreds of songs, we find ourselves listening to the same ones. Why? It's the same reason we might choose the same type of partners or fall into old habits. They're familiar. Our brain loves what it knows. Imagine it like walking a well-worn path in a forest. Even if it's not the best or safest path, it's the one we know, so we stick to it.

For me, I often found myself with partners who let me down. Not on purpose, but it felt easier. I saw parts of myself in them, and honestly, getting to know someone new felt like a lot of work. Deep down, I had this nagging feeling that maybe I didn't deserve better. So, I kept walking that same path.

This is why some of us might go back to an ex, even if we know they're not right for us. Trying a new path or a new relationship feels uncertain. It's stepping into the unknown. But sometimes, the unknown could be the very place we find what we're truly looking for.

Repetitive compulsion gives birth to the unconscious commitment we often make to repeating unhelpful patterns. Once we get to the chapter on thriving in this book, we will have the strength to let go of these commitments. They may have served you well in the past. For example, having rigid boundaries after a breakup is normal and expected, as we talked about in hermit mode, but if you keep them rigid long enough, they might turn into emotional walls. Our process of healing is intended to guide us toward a time where we no longer need these commitments and can let go of the compulsion to repeat them.

What does this mean for our relationships? We often choose what's familiar even if it's unsafe because we know what to expect. It feels as though we're securing what we missed growing up, or at least attempting to right the story.

For example, if you grew up in a home where love, attention, and affection from a parent wasn't readily available, you might find yourself in an unhealthy relationship with someone who also withholds love, seeking the love you missed. Again, this pattern of emotional unavailability is familiar to you, so it feels "safe." Perhaps you tried to earn love by performing or auditioning for it because the message you received is you weren't worthy otherwise. Feeling lovable as you are without having to work for it amid uncertainty and volatility might even seem strange to you. You might have a hard time believing in this love when it is given to you due to the lurking toxic shame you have around your worthiness.

The other side of this is that while you're seeking the love you missed, you've also learned to expect very little of it. This is why you might people-please and/or accept breadcrumbs of attention and approval in your platonic, romantic, or professional relationships in order to secure acceptance. For many of my clients, acceptance and approval feel like the love they always needed, even if it was rarely expressed in this way growing up. So while you may be seeking what you missed, you are doing exactly that—seeking the very little love, attention, and affection that you are used to. Your brain learned to normalize this as a reference point for what to expect in relationships.

These relationships are rarely healthy and eventually erupt in turmoil down the line. Due to this underlying dysfunction, the people you choose aren't equipped to give you the love you missed and ultimately need—unless they're doing their own inner work. So you end up back where you started: seeking partners who perpetuate unhealthy patterns of relating that repeat cycles of trauma as you relive your childhood in survival mode.

And keep in mind, none of this is your fault. Much of this is unconscious until we become aware enough to garner the necessary insights that then set the stage for change. Healing isn't simply a tool for survival, it's a practice that will help you return to your authentic self.

Over the years, I've had many clients exhibit these patterns, but I always return to one client in particular: Morgan. Her story shows how these past familial dynamics often play out in our romantic relationships. As you read the following, note where you've either engaged in similar behavior or you were the recipient of it.

Morgan was in her mid-thirties and had a pattern of intense, volatile relationships. She was always chasing after that intense chemistry and emotional volatility that came with them. During our first session, she shared with me how she would obsess over her new partners, romanticize them, and love-bomb them with all her might.

"I just need to feel that connection," she said, "and if I don't, I move on."

It was clear to me that Morgan's preoccupation with her partners was her way of feeling loved and chosen. It was her survival mode, her way of coping with the fear of being alone. But this way of coping was not healthy, and it was taking a toll on her.

Morgan's emotional volatility was another red flag. She would go from love-bombing her partners to breadcrumbing and ghosting them, creating intense emotional highs and lows. When she felt uncertain about her partner's intentions, she would initiate push-pull behavior to maintain control. It was like she was living on autopilot, reactive to her partners' actions, neglecting self-care and other activities.

From our sessions, I observed Morgan avoid emotional connections because they felt too intense and overwhelming. Her disconnection manifested in drug and alcohol abuse, and emotionally addictive relationships. She would distract herself with romanticizing and fantasizing to avoid the pain after a breakup. Morgan's insecurity and low self-worth were evident in her comparison to her friends and her partners' exes. She would chronically people-please, abandoning herself and betraying her values to secure love, attention, and affection.

During our therapy sessions, Morgan and I delved into her past and the origins of her coping mechanisms. As we unwound the layers, several moments stood out:

Mindfulness Techniques: In one of our sessions, Morgan took a deep breath and tried a simple mindfulness exercise. With every breath, she felt a wave of calmness she wasn't used to. It was like opening an old photo album; she realized that her rush for love and validation echoed the quiet loneliness of her childhood. That stillness made her recognize the distractions she used to mask her feelings around the emotional neglect she experienced as a child.

Identifying Emotions: During a therapy session, we worked on naming what she felt during certain memories. Morgan's eyes lit up when she realized that the "fear" she often felt in relationships was the same unease she felt as a child around her unpredictable dad. It's like she found missing pieces of a puzzle, making sense of why she sought relationships that mirrored the emotional chaos of her early life.

Building Self-Worth: As Morgan wrote down moments when she felt she compromised too much in relationships, she remembered molding herself into someone she thought her parents would love more. Those memories helped her see that her pattern of people-pleasing started way back when she tried to be the "good kid" just to get a little more attention and love.

Emotional Role-Play: During an emotional role-play, Morgan's reactions felt eerily similar to her childhood—those days when she tiptoed around her parents, trying to gauge their moods. She saw that her push-pull actions with partners weren't just random; they were a replay of her early attempts to control an unpredictable home environment.

Reframing Her Past: Morgan began to view her past through a more understanding and compassionate lens. When she reflected on a particularly difficult breakup, memories of her childhood resurfaced—times when she had to summon inner strength. Gradually, a pattern became evident: her tendency to dive into passionate relationships was her way of re-creating the tumultuous emotions she experienced growing up.

Through these examples and many sessions together, Morgan began to grasp how her past traumas and coping mechanisms had shaped her current behavior. It was a challenging journey, but with each session, she took a step closer to breaking her patterns and embracing a healthier approach to relationships.

Morgan gradually learned to become more present and accept her emotions without judgment. She learned to set boundaries and communicate her needs with her partners. Over time, Morgan started to let go of her old patterns and embrace healthier ways of coping. She learned to love and accept herself, and in turn, she started choosing healthier relationships. Morgan's journey was beautiful to witness. She learned to live in the middle ground, away from the extremes of emotional volatility and avoidance. That, my dears, is what true healing is all about.

During our sessions, Morgan and I comfortably settled into sharing and exploring her roller-coaster relationships. With a soft sigh and a distant gaze, she explained, "There's this rush of excitement and passion that just . . . makes me feel so alive, you know?"

Digging a bit deeper into the rough patches of these relationships, Morgan hesitated before sharing, "It gets tough. The fear of losing someone, the anxiety . . . I just react, sometimes impulsively."

As the memories of her past began to flow, Morgan opened up about her unpredictable mother, drawing an unintended parallel between the inconsistent love in her childhood and her patterns in adult relationships.

Gently reflecting on her past, Morgan's voice quivered. "I've always looked for that intensity, that chaos in relationships. Maybe it's my way of filling that childhood void. But deep down, what I've been longing for is stability, consistency, and genuine emotional connection."

Morgan's story resonated with a pattern I'd seen before. It was as if she'd been on autopilot, drawn subconsciously to the familiarity of her tumultuous past. This survival instinct, a deeply ingrained mechanism to seek out immediate emotional safety, had Morgan mistaking fleeting moments of attention for genuine, lasting connection. There was this pattern, almost an addiction to the ebb and flow of her relationships. It provided a temporary high, a short-lived escape from deeper, lingering issues. This cycle, although comforting in its familiarity, was inadvertently toxic.

The challenge—and beauty—of therapy lies in gently guiding clients like Morgan to see these patterns. It's not always clear cut, and that's okay. Many of us are in this unintentional "survival mode," just getting by. But living on the edge and constantly reacting can sometimes lead us astray. Recognizing this and understanding it can be the first step toward healing and genuine connection.

My goal is to help my clients see this and begin to develop a greater sense of self-awareness and emotional regulation as they heal. Sarah learned to recognize when she was falling back into old patterns, and therefore make different choices based on what she truly needed and wanted.

By learning to live more authentically and prioritizing our own needs and desires, we can break free from the cycle of dysfunction in relationships. By moving out of survival mode and into a space of self-regulation and healing, we begin to attract partners who are able to meet our needs and create healthy, fulfilling connections. This is what makes the healing journey about returning home to ourselves. Maybe we can't solve our problems overnight, but we can engage in activities that allow us to be mindful of what's happening in our heart, mind, and body.

But there's one thing that often prevents us from leaving this behind: toxic shame.

WHAT IS TOXIC SHAME?

Toxic shame, at its heart, is that lingering feeling that, deep down, there's something fundamentally wrong with us, even if there's no clear reason to feel that way. It's like an internal voice that whispers, "You're not good enough," or "You're unlovable," regardless of what the world outside tells us. It's not about the mistakes we make or the times we stumble; it's more about an ingrained belief that our very essence is flawed. It's important to remember, though, that while these feelings might be deeply rooted, they don't define our worth or potential. Recognizing them is the first step toward healing and self-love.

For the survivors of relational trauma, all of this feels very real, even if it isn't. Consequently, our core task when healing after relational trauma is to heal the shame that sits silently at our core, fueling a life grounded in survival mode.

To fully identify and stamp out this dangerous internal talk, we need to understand the difference between healthy shame and toxic shame.

Healthy Shame: Think of healthy shame as a gentle internal reminder that we're human and imperfect. It nudges us, saying, "Hey, maybe that wasn't the best choice," and it encourages us to recognize our boundaries and limitations. Healthy shame can serve as a form of protection, ensuring that we don't overstep or harm ourselves and others. It's a way for our conscience to guide us in our relationships and actions, promoting personal growth.

Toxic Shame: On the other hand, toxic shame feels heavier and all-consuming. It's not just about our actions, but it takes a toll on our very identity. Instead of saying, "I made a mistake," it whispers, "I *am* a mistake." It's the pervasive feeling that we are fundamentally flawed or unlovable, often stemming from past traumas or deeply ingrained beliefs. Over time, this can hinder our self-worth, relationships, and overall well-being.

Keeping all of this in mind, it's common for us to confuse feelings of shame with those of guilt. Consider this scenario in the context of a toxic or codependent relationship: Imagine you forget your partner's birthday. If you're feeling guilt, you recognize the action—forgetting the date—as the issue. You might think, "I made a mistake and need to apologize." But if you're feeling shame, it's more like thinking, "I'm a terrible partner and person because I forgot."

By understanding this difference, you can pinpoint that what you're really feeling is guilt about an oversight, rather than internalize it as a reflection of your self-worth. This recognition can be pivotal. It allows you to address behaviors, like forgetting important dates, without spiraling into self-deprecation. And in the context of healing from codependency, it promotes self-compassion and accountability, rather than getting trapped in a cycle of self-blame.

Shame is more about self-evaluation, and it's internalized. It's the feeling that there's something wrong with us as a person. Phrases like "I am bad" or "I am unworthy" are rooted in shame. While shame can sometimes serve as a social regulator, when it becomes overwhelming, it's challenging to address the root cause and move forward.

Guilt, conversely, is about our actions. It's the recognition that we might have done something wrong. If shame says, "I am bad," guilt says, "I did something bad." It's a natural feeling that arises when we think we've caused harm or broken a personal or societal rule. Guilt can be constructive, pushing us to make amends, apologize, or change our behavior.

In essence, while these emotions might be uncomfortable, they offer valuable insights into our inner world. Recognizing the differences between them allows us to address our feelings more effectively, cultivating understanding and self-compassion.

HOW TOXIC SHAME FUELS SURVIVAL MODE

To truly understand the nuances of survival mode, it's imperative to explore its deep-seated connection with toxic shame. At its core, survival mode is our body's primal response to danger; it's about keeping us safe in the face of threats. But when we marinate in feelings of toxic shame, we're constantly on alert, perceiving threats even in everyday situations.

Why? Because toxic shame convinces us of our inherent

unworthiness, making us hypersensitive to judgment or criticism, and triggering that fight-or-flight response. When we operate from this heightened state, we're more likely to see ourselves through a distorted lens, one tainted by that ingrained feeling of being "not good enough." To step out of survival mode, it's essential to shed the heavy cloak of toxic shame. By understanding and healing the sources of this shame, we give ourselves a chance to live fully, beyond mere survival.

Here are a few examples of sources of toxic shame that fuel survival mode:

Trauma or Abuse: Experiences like sexual abuse or assault, whether in childhood or adulthood, can implant profound feelings of toxic shame. This can sometimes cause a painful repetition of past violations, each repetition further embedding that shame.

Shaming in Childhood: During formative years, many children encounter shaming, often from well-meaning parents or caregivers trying to mold their behavior. Comments like "Little boys don't cry!" or "You're making Mommy sad!" might unintentionally warp a child's self-perception, affecting how they relate to others and themselves.

Relational Trauma: Emotional and verbal abuse within relationships can instill a sense of shame, especially when partners belittle basic emotional needs or deny one's experiences.

Unresolved Core Wounding: Sometimes, we carry shame

from sources we can't even pinpoint. These hidden wounds can deeply impact our self-view and reactions.

Society and Culture: Society and culture are like silent narrators, gently weaving stories about who we should be and how we should act. These narratives don't just set guidelines; they paint vivid pictures of our self-worth, belonging, and place in the world.

    Race: Our world, rich in diverse cultures and histories, unfortunately still carries lingering racial stereotypes and biases. These can sometimes cause people from certain racial backgrounds to feel like they're in the shadows, overlooked or misunderstood because of their skin color. Such feelings can be deeply internalized, leading to a quiet, painful sense of shame.

    Gender: Over time, societies have crafted specific roles for men and women. While many of these roles have their roots in care and tradition, they can also limit self-expression. When someone doesn't align perfectly with these expectations, they might feel a gentle tug of being "different" or "not fitting in."

    Sexual Orientation: Love, in all its forms, is beautiful. Yet, some societies still have a narrow lens through which they view love and relationships. For those whose hearts beat differently, there can be an unspoken burden, a silent weight of feeling "othered" merely for seeking genuine connection.

    Class: Economic backgrounds tell stories of struggles, triumphs, privileges, and challenges. Often, people from varying economic statuses feel the subtle gaze of society, measuring our worth in material terms. Whether you come from a place of plenty or a place of want, societal perceptions can sometimes cause us to question our worth and place.

Religious Expectations: Faith and religious institutions can have stringent expectations around obedience. When these aren't met or specific rules are breached, we might grapple with intense feelings of shame.

Toxic shame blends into our survival instincts, influencing our choices, especially in love and relationships. It can stem from past experiences or even societal norms. But there's hope—acknowledging the roots of toxic shame can pave the way for deeper understanding and healing. As we move forward, we'll delve into how this plays out in our dating lives.

TOXIC SHAME IN OUR DATING LIVES

In the intricate dance of dating and relationships, toxic shame can often cast a shadow over our choices. Picture someone, a friend or even a reflection of our past selves, who yearns for a steadfast, meaningful relationship. Yet, time and again, they find themselves entangled in fleeting moments, brief encounters, or relationships that don't fully align with what their heart truly seeks. This is not a judgment of these decisions, but rather an invitation to reflect: "Is this the connection I genuinely desire, or am I trying to fill a void?"

This journey for love and acceptance isn't always straightforward. Some of us, eager for any semblance of warmth and closeness, might extend our boundaries beyond what feels right. We compromise, sacrificing our innermost needs for a momentary connection or a hint of affection. But on the flip side, there are those who, having been hurt before, have built walls so high that they find it difficult to let anyone in, to really share that vulnerable part of themselves.

At the core of these dynamics is often a misalignment between our external actions and internal desires. We might tell ourselves stories about what we want in our romantic and platonic relationships, in our careers, or even in our daily interactions. "Maybe this is what I deserve," we might think, or "This is as good as it gets." Past choices linger like ghosts, bringing along baggage like guilt or regret. And what about the pressures? Oh, they're ever-present: the need to fit into a mold, whether it's about age, appearance, career trajectory, or societal expectations. All the while, a nagging doubt lingers: "Am I a fraud?" or "Will they see through me?"

For some, finding solace might mean turning to distractions—habits or activities that numb the pain or create a temporary escape. For others, it could mean steering clear of true intimacy, guarding their hearts against potential hurt. Beneath this all, a quiet voice sometimes murmurs those deep-seated fears: "Maybe I'm not lovable," "I'll always be on the outskirts, looking in," or "Why do I always feel not quite 'enough'?"

These feelings, while heavy, are also a testament to our shared human experience. By shining a light on them, and by understanding and embracing them with kindness, we pave the way for healing and authentic attachments.

8

. . . .

Decoding Attachment Styles

t's said that "time heals all wounds," but in reality, the passing of time can force you to accept living with the pain and shame created by unresolved trauma. It insidiously seeps into your relationships, disconnecting you from yourself in order to survive it.

As we discussed in the previous chapter, this is why you might end up repeating the same patterns: entering the same toxic relationships with the same type of person, trying but failing to achieve certain goals, and remaining mired in a failure-to-launch state, resulting in frequent crises. You might also find yourself perpetuating and passing down generational trauma because it's all you've known. Automatic negative thoughts give you all the reasons you shouldn't let people in, fed by the beliefs you have about yourself from unresolved trauma.

And at the center of all of this is toxic shame. For survivors of relational trauma, the manifestation of toxic shame—insecurity, guilt, regret, self-loathing, and negative thinking patterns—can feel all too real. Healing the shame that sits at your core is essential for stepping out of survival mode and recovering after relational trauma.

ATTACHMENT STYLES
AND TRAUMA RESPONSES

Navigating our emotional landscape can be likened to embarking on a journey, where every step we take is influenced by our early experiences and the beliefs we've formed about ourselves. As we reflect on the weight of toxic shame, it's essential to recognize that these deep-seated emotions and beliefs, known as core wounds, not only shape our perceptions but also influence how we connect with others. Think of these connections as intricate dances, and in these dances, our patterns, our rhythm—our attachment styles—come to light.

Attachment styles, in essence, describe our patterns of bonding, connecting, and relating to others. Rooted in our earliest relationships, usually with caregivers or parents, these styles provide a framework for understanding how we respond to closeness, intimacy, and vulnerability in relationships. There are two major types of attachment styles: secure and insecure. Those with insecure attachment styles, such as anxious or avoidant attachment styles, are often triggered when in romantic relationships, as they have not properly worked through childhood wounds. Those with a secure attachment style, though by no means perfect in the area of love, tend to be able to face their triggers and work collaboratively with their partner to develop a healthy love that sidesteps toxicity and codependency. Here are some descriptions of a few of the more common attachment styles:

The **secure attachment style** is characterized by a healthy balance of independence and connection. These people feel confident in their relationships and are able to express their needs and emotions without fear of rejection. They are also able to support and comfort their partners when needed.

The **anxious-preoccupied attachment style** is characterized by a strong desire for closeness and connection, but a lack of trust in others. These individuals may be overly dependent on their partners and may struggle with feelings of insecurity and anxiety. They may also have a tendency to be controlling or jealous in their relationships.

The **dismissive-avoidant attachment style** is characterized by a desire for independence and a fear of being vulnerable or intimate with others. These individuals may struggle with feelings of inadequacy and may avoid close relationships or minimize the importance of attachment.

The **fearful-avoidant attachment style** is characterized by a fear of both intimacy and isolation. Individuals with this attachment style may struggle with trusting others and have difficulty forming close relationships. They may also have a tendency to be emotionally distant or unavailable.

The **disorganized attachment style** is characterized by an inconsistent and unpredictable approach to relationships. Those with a disorganized attachment style may experience intense and conflicting emotions in relationships, including both a desire for intimacy and a fear of being hurt or rejected. They may also struggle

with trusting others and regulating their own emotions,
leading to difficulties communicating or maintaining
healthy relationships.

CORE WOUNDS, ATTACHMENT STYLES, AND TRAUMA RESPONSES

As you navigate the intricate landscape of relationships, echoes
from your past reverberate, shaping your attachment styles and
uncovering your core wounds. These deep-seated beliefs, perhaps telling you "I am unlovable" or "I am not enough," play a
crucial role in how you connect and respond to others. When
you delve deeper, you'll see how these core wounds don't just
influence your attachment style; they also manifest in your
interactions, sometimes leading you into the ambiguous realm
of situationships.

Picture a situationship as an undefined space where you
find yourself entangled, driven by a desire for validation and
acceptance. Your craving for reassurance and worth, deeply
rooted in negative core wounds, transforms the situationship
into a stage where old patterns replay and unhealed wounds
come back to the surface. For instance, the ambiguity and lack
of commitment can trigger your intense fears of abandonment,
reflecting and reinforcing the belief that you're not worth committing to or staying for.

This intricate connection between situationships, core
wounds, and attachment styles becomes vivid in your responses
to situations and people. As a people-pleaser, you might find

yourself caught in a struggle between standing up for your needs and succumbing to the desire to be accepted, navigating the stormy seas of toxic shame rooted in core wounds of unworthiness. This toxic shame, like a haunting melody in the background, fuels your cycle of seeking validation, tolerating ambiguity, and struggling with boundary setting—all hallmarks of situationships.

Conversely, if your attachment style leans toward avoidant, possibly carrying the core wound of "I don't matter," you may find yourself in a situationship as a way to maintain distance and avoid vulnerability. If you're more anxiously attached and haunted by the fear of not being enough, the uncertainty of a situationship can be simultaneously agonizing and familiar, a reflection of your deepest fears and beliefs about yourself.

Your core wounds can manifest not just in your attachment styles but in your thoughts, feelings, and behaviors, leading to obsessive thoughts as an avoidance tactic to escape the emotional pain. They follow you like shadows, influencing your reactions within relationships, from feeling rejected and abandoned to feeling invisible and unworthy.

Navigating through the intricacies of core wounds, attachment styles, and situationships might seem like a complex dance, but you're already on the right track by acknowledging and exploring these patterns. You're essentially peeling back the layers, getting to the heart of the old beliefs and automatic responses that have been running the show, perhaps for quite some time.

This is your moment to breathe, to understand, and to choose a different path. It's about making connections between your past experiences and your present reality, all with the intention of building stronger, healthier relationships and finding a sense of peace within yourself.

You might be wondering, "What's next? How do I navigate through all of this?" Well, that's where we'll dive into understanding trauma responses. These responses are your body and mind's way of protecting you, like an internal security system. But sometimes, they can get a bit overzealous, especially when old wounds and shame are in the mix.

In the next part of our journey together, we'll explore these trauma responses in more detail—understanding how they show up, what triggers them, and most important, how you can navigate through them. The fight, flight, fawn, and freeze responses are all part of your natural defense mechanisms, but understanding them is key to making sure they serve you in the best way possible. So, let's navigate through these responses, empowering you to take control and find a sense of calm amid the complexity.

Trauma responses are natural and normal ways for our brains and bodies to react to dangerous or overwhelming situations, but they can also be triggered by unresolved emotional trauma and toxic shame. Here are some of the most common responses:

The fight response is characterized by aggression and the desire to attack or confront the source of shame. This can manifest as anger, defensiveness, or even violence. While it may provide a temporary sense of power or control, the fight response can escalate situations and lead to further harm or conflict.

The flight response involves fleeing or avoiding the source of shame altogether. This can take the form of substance abuse, escapism through media, or even physical distance. While it may provide temporary relief, the flight response does not address the root causes of our shame and can lead to further isolation and disconnection from others.

The fawn response involves trying to please or appease others in an effort to avoid shame. This can manifest as people-pleasing, codependency, or sacrificing one's own needs for the sake of others. While it may temporarily avoid shame, the fawn response can lead to the erosion of one's sense of self and the development of unhealthy relationships.

The freeze response involves shutting down or numbing out in the face of shame. This can manifest as dissociation, avoidance, or a lack of emotional response. While it may provide temporary relief, the freeze response does not allow us to process or address our emotions, leading to a buildup of unresolved trauma.

If any of these behaviors resonate, it can be a hint toward the kind of trauma response you're most likely to engage with. It's important to be gentle with yourself as you work toward healing and resolving any underlying emotional trauma. These responses are not inherently bad or wrong. They are natural survival mechanisms that can serve a purpose in certain situations. However, when they are fueled by toxic shame, they can become unhealthy and destructive.

While these trauma responses can be helpful in protecting you in the short-term, they can also be damaging if they become habitual or if you are unable to resolve the underlying emotional trauma that is driving them. When you are constantly in survival mode, it can be difficult to live a healthy and fulfilling life, as your energy and focus are constantly directed toward avoiding danger or conflict.

Another way you might manage the internal conflicts around connection and acceptance is by developing an insecure attachment style. As a child, you were completely dependent on your caregiver for survival. This created an attachment bond that formed the foundation for all your future relationships. If the bond was strong and secure, you would have developed a healthy sense of attachment that would allow you to feel confident and secure in your relationships.

However, if this bond was disrupted or broken, it could lead to unresolved attachment trauma. This might have occurred if you had a caregiver who was consistently unavailable, inconsistent, or neglectful. As a result, you may have developed one of four attachment styles: secure, anxious-preoccupied, dismissive-avoidant, or fearful-avoidant.

When you struggle to manage trauma responses and insecure attachment styles, you focus less on connection and more on transaction in order to get your needs met. Relational trauma disconnects you from your core emotional needs around emotional safety, consistency, validation, and connections that are authentic, healthy, and conscious.

What this may look like for you in the present is a lack of boundaries; you might be people-pleasing and over-functioning in relationships by seeking your partner's love and approval because you're anxious and preoccupied with the fate of the relationship. You equate your partner's love and approval with safety.

Let's look at this hypothetical example: your partner is late picking you up from the airport. You feel extremely anxious, or even rageful, since their tardiness reminds you of the chronic lateness of your caregiver in picking you up after school. It goes deeper than just being late. This experience conjures the anxiety around feeling abandoned and uncared for, a feeling that stemmed from your childhood, when you didn't have a voice or even feel that you had a right to express these feelings. Today, this shows up as a fight response, along with an anxious attachment style.

You might think nothing of this, but your brain continues to live in fear of abandonment. Being disconnected from a parent, caregiver, or secure attachment figure due to inconsistent care, absent validation, or emotional neglect can feel like death. As an adult, you will unconsciously frame your partner as a secure home base. When they show up with behavior that feels like abandonment, you might experience a trauma response.

Someone with a secure attachment style might note the reaction, self-soothe, and consider the possibility that their partner might simply be stuck in traffic. With a fight response, you might resort to yelling in an effort to control your partner's behavior. You may not intend for this to be hurtful, but in order to ensure that you don't feel abandoned again, you might do this thinking it'll guarantee they're on time in the future.

Your relationship then becomes a hotbed of emotional volatility teeming with resentment, anger, and frustration, with neither partner's needs being met. In part, this is because you're not aware of why you feel the way you do, and thus you're unable to have the difficult conversations around your attachment styles. It isn't that a secure and consciously loving relationship won't have issues. They do have issues, but as you dive deeper on your healing journey, you gain the tools to address them in a manner that isn't harmful or threatening.

It's important to recognize that these attachment styles are not set in stone and can change over time with the right support and healing tools. Empathy, validation, and having difficult conversations is an important part of the repair process in relationships, and it requires insight into how your past shows up today. Otherwise, your relationships exist solely as a means to avoid unresolved emotional issues from the past. This is how living in survival mode gives birth to other toxic situations, like codependency and transactional relationships. But most people—like most relationships—are not straightforward. Trauma responses can intersect with attachment styles, leading to many complex combinations of behaviors and reactions. But even these "cocktails" can be figured out with enough attention.

THE COCKTAIL OF TRAUMA RESPONSES AND ATTACHMENT STYLES

There are several possible permutations of trauma responses and attachment styles. These combinations will impact how you understand what's actually creating chaos and confusion in your relationships (often not what you think it is!), how to recognize the patterns before they turn things upside down, and why the romantic situations you're in can feel unpredictable and tumultuous. These are typically the main categories:

Fawn-Anxious: May have learned to cope with trauma by prioritizing the needs and desires of others, often at the expense of their own well-being; highly empathetic and attuned to others' emotions. This type may struggle to set boundaries or assert their own needs.

Freeze-Anxious: May have learned to cope with trauma by dissociating or "checking out" from their environment; struggles connecting with others emotionally, appearing detached or aloof.

Flight-Anxious: May have learned to cope with trauma by avoiding or fleeing from situations that trigger anxiety or fear; highly avoidant of conflict and struggles to confront challenges head-on.

Fight-Anxious: May have learned to cope with trauma by becoming highly reactive or defensive in response to perceived threats; quick to anger. This type has difficulty regulating emotions in stressful situations.

Fawn-Fearful: May have experienced trauma that has left them feeling powerless or vulnerable; may have feelings of inadequacy and low self-worth. This type is highly dependent on others for validation and support.

Freeze-Fearful: May have experienced trauma that has left them feeling overwhelmed or unable to cope; feelings of helplessness or hopelessness. This type may withdraw from others as a way of self-protection.

Flight-Fearful: May have experienced trauma that has left them feeling unsafe or threatened; may be highly avoidant of situations or people that they perceive as potential sources of danger and struggle to trust others.

Fight-Fearful: May have experienced trauma that has left them feeling powerless or victimized; highly reactive or defensive. This type may have difficulty regulating emotions in response to stress or conflict.

Fawn-Dismissive: May have learned to cope with trauma by avoiding emotional intimacy or vulnerability. This type prioritizes independence and self-reliance and may struggle to form deep, meaningful relationships with others.

Freeze-Dismissive: May have learned to cope with trauma by emotionally disconnecting from others; doesn't like to rely on others for support or comfort.

Flight-Dismissive: May have learned to cope with trauma by avoiding emotional connection or commitment; highly avoidant of situations that require emotional vulnerability. This type may prioritize their own needs over the needs of others.

Fight-Dismissive: May have learned to cope with trauma by becoming aggressive or dominant in social situations. This type might prioritize power or control and struggle to connect with others emotionally.

Fawn-Disorganized: May have experienced trauma that has left them feeling confused or disoriented; struggles with emotional regulation, exhibiting unpredictable or contradictory patterns of behavior.

Freeze-Disorganized: May have experienced trauma that has left them feeling disconnected or alienated from their environment; struggles to maintain a sense of self or identity. This type may feel detached or numb.

Flight-Disorganized: May exhibit erratic behavior and emotional dysregulation, often using aggression or impulsivity as means of control. This type is characterized by a blend of avoidant and anxious behaviors, leading to difficulties in forming stable, secure relationships. It results from a mix of the disorganized attachment pattern and a flight response to perceived threats, manifesting in inconsistent and unpredictable behavior.

Fight-Disorganized: May have experienced trauma that has left them feeling overwhelmed or threatened; may exhibit aggressive or impulsive behavior as a way of asserting control over their environment. This type may have difficulty with emotional regulation and consistent or predictable behavior. They also might struggle with attachment and forming stable relationships with others.

Let's take a look at some examples of how these combinations might play out in real life:

The Fight-Anxious Archetype

When the fight trauma response and anxious attachment style combine, this can create a specific way of behaving in relationships. The fight response often manifests in aggressive or defensive behavior and is triggered by feeling threatened or

vulnerable. With an anxious attachment style, you crave closeness and intimacy but also fear abandonment and rejection.

When these two parts combine, it can look like constantly
seeking reassurance from your partner, while also being quick
to anger or react defensively when you feel insecure. You may
become jealous or possessive, demand constant attention or
affection, and become angry or aggressive if you feel like your
needs are not being met. Consequently, this can lead to a lot
of conflict and tension in your relationship, as your partner
may feel overwhelmed or suffocated by your constant need for
reassurance and reactivity.

This was the case with Ava, a client of mine who struggled
with the fight trauma response and anxious attachment style.
She began by telling me about a recent fight she'd had with her
partner. "It was like everything he said just triggered me," she
explained. "I felt like he was attacking me, and I had to defend
myself."

As she spoke, I could see the tension in her body, the tightness
in her jaw, and the anger in her eyes. I knew that this was a common experience for Ava. She had a tendency to see everything as
a potential threat, and her fight response would kick in before she
had a chance to really think about what was happening.

I asked her to describe the fight in more detail, and she
shared how she had accused her partner of not caring about
her and threatened to leave the relationship. When I asked
what had triggered her, she revealed that her partner had been
spending more time with his friends lately, and she felt like she
was being pushed to the side.

We talked about how her anxiety around abandonment was

driving her reaction, and how her fight response was making the situation worse. As we explored Ava's childhood experiences, she shared with me that she grew up in a household where her parents fought constantly. This created an environment of instability, and she often felt anxious and on edge as a child.

Additionally, Ava's parents were emotionally unavailable, and she felt neglected and unimportant. These experiences left Ava feeling like she always had to be on high alert and fight for attention and love. As she grew up, she internalized these experiences and began to believe that the only way to get what she wanted was through fighting and creating chaos.

Ava's attachment style was also heavily influenced by her childhood experiences. She had an anxious attachment style, which meant that she craved closeness and validation from her partner but also felt a constant fear of abandonment. This made her prone to reacting strongly in her relationships, especially when she felt that her partner was pulling away or not giving her the attention she desired.

All of these experiences and patterns in Ava's life created a self-perpetuating cycle. Her anxious attachment style made her more likely to overreact in her relationships, which then fueled her fight trauma response, making her more reactive and aggressive.

As we delved deeper into our sessions, Ava and I started unearthing layers of her past, sifting through memories that had long been dormant. The journey was akin to piecing together a puzzle; with each memory, the picture became clearer.

"You know," she began one day, her voice reflecting a mix of apprehension and curiosity, "I remember how my father would raise his voice over the smallest of things. And every time he did, I would shrink into my shell, hoping to become invisible."

I nodded, urging her to continue.

"And then there were the times my mother would shut down completely, not speaking to anyone for days. It felt like walking on eggshells around her," Ava added, her eyes distant.

Drawing the parallels became an enlightening experience for her. Ava's partner had certain habits that inadvertently mirrored those of her parents. A loud tone or a period of silence, even if it wasn't directed at her, would catapult her back to her childhood, triggering feelings of insecurity and defense.

"It's like I'm that little girl all over again, trying to shield herself from the chaos around her," she remarked. This realization was poignant. Ava's reactions to her partner were, in many ways, a defense mechanism she'd developed as a child to cope with the unpredictable environment she'd grown up in.

We spent time reflecting on these patterns, discussing how the child in her was still trying to protect the adult Ava. "But I'm not that helpless child anymore," she said determinedly in one of our sessions. And she was right. Recognizing the origin of her reactions was the first step. Now, she had the tools and awareness to reshape them, to respond rather than react, and to build bridges instead of walls in her relationship.

This newfound understanding was transformative for Ava. It not only provided clarity about her past but also illuminated the path for a more conscious and intentional future with her partner.

One area we delved deeply into was recognizing and managing triggers. Every person has a "jump-off" point—a physiological sign that indicates they're about to be overwhelmed or triggered. For some, it might be clammy hands, for others a tight chest or a peculiar numbness in the head.

Identifying this "jump-off" point became Ava's first line of defense. By becoming hyperaware of her body's cues, she could gauge when she was entering triggered territory, enabling her to take proactive steps to calm down.

Once she had identified her "jump-off" point, we then explored a step-by-step approach to self-soothing:

Physical Grounding: Try stamping your feet on the ground, clenching and unclenching fists, or holding on to a piece of furniture. This helps reconnect with the present and diverts the mind momentarily.

Short Burst Activities: Engage in activities like jumping jacks or a brisk walk. Physical movement can release some of that pent-up energy, facilitating a transition into a calmer state.

Transition to Deep Breathing: Once you're slightly calmer, deep breathing comes into play. Start with shallow breaths, gradually deepening them. Visualize inhaling serenity and exhaling tension.

Positive Affirmations: As Ava found her rhythm in calming down, positive affirmations became a powerful tool. Phrases like "I am calm and in control" proved invaluable once the initial intensity had subsided.

A few days after our detailed exploration of these techniques, Ava walked into our session radiating a newfound energy. With evident pride, she recounted a recent encounter with her partner. She had not only managed to articulate her feelings but did so without resorting to defensiveness or aggression. The techniques we discussed had made a palpable difference, and she was visibly proud of her strides.

While there was still work to be done, Ava was making progress. Together, we continued to explore the root causes of her attachment style and trauma response, and worked on building healthier patterns in her relationships.

The Fawn-Anxious Archetype

This is a hybrid of the fawn trauma response and anxious attachment. You tend to alternate between conflict and caretaking, people-pleasing, or fawning around your partner to keep the peace or reconcile after conflict.

This type vacillates between intense conflict and caretaking or people-pleasing while also maintaining covert control of their partner and the relationship.

This type may use caretaking in a covertly coercive and manipulative way that feels insincere to their partner. This can look like love-bombing after a conflict to smooth things over and shove their issues under the rug. As the child of a high conflict, emotionally abusive, or neglectful parent, this type learned to acquiesce to another's needs in order to avoid conflict and keep the peace.

However, the preoccupation with the relationship can create the very conflict they're also trying to avoid. They may sometimes do this via long monologues amid conflict, intense phone or text contact, or long, drawn-out arguments to emotionally beat their partners into submission. When making attempts to reconcile, they will self-abandon to keep the peace, often to the extreme of resentful servitude which eventually erupts into another volatile conflict down the road.

This type may also play the role of both victim and abuser while using conflict to create and feel connection. For example, they may start an argument to test the waters, seeing whether their partner will leave. If the partner doesn't leave, they've successfully tested their limits. If they do leave, this sets the stage for more conflict as they work (read: fawn) to get their partner to reconcile.

While in the fawn (people-pleasing) space, this type is often exploited due to playing the "nice" role, which ultimately results in declarations of being a victim in the relationship. And while this is often true, in their determination to take back control they switch to the role of abuser in order to maintain control.

At the core of anxious attachment is the belief that one is unworthy of love and connection. As a result, those with anxious attachment often seek constant reassurance and validation from their partners, and may become overly dependent on them for emotional support. This can lead to high levels of conflict and reactivity, becoming jealous, possessive, and prone to seeking attention and approval from their partners. In an effort to keep the relationship from being derailed due to what can feel like an unconscious, insatiable need for conflict, the fawn response takes over.

The fawn trauma response is a pattern that involves suppressing one's own needs and desires in order to placate or appease others. It is often triggered by experiences of abuse, trauma, or other forms of adversity, and is characterized by a lack of assertiveness and a tendency to "go along" with others in order to avoid conflict or maintain relationships.

The combination of these two attachment styles can be particularly challenging. You might oscillate between feelings of anxiety and a desire to please or appease your partner in order to maintain the relationship. This can lead to a cycle of conflict and caretaking, as you may feel constantly torn between your own needs and desires and the needs of your partner.

Despite these challenges, it is important to remember that everyone has the capacity to change and grow. With the right support and guidance, those with the fawn-anxious archetype can learn to regulate their emotions and build healthier, more fulfilling relationships. This may involve seeking attachment-focused psychotherapy, learning new coping strategies, or working to develop a greater sense of self-worth and self-acceptance.

In the cozy corner of my office, surrounded by sunlit plants and the gentle hum of the outside world, I leaned back, thinking about Clara's journey, a prime example of the fawn-anxious dance.

"Okay, so, Clara," I started, chuckling a bit and using my hands to gesture as if I was choreographing a dance. "Imagine your emotional life is like this . . . a bit of a salsa dance."

She raised an eyebrow, a hint of a smile playing on her lips. "A salsa? Really?"

I nodded enthusiastically. "Yep! On one end, you've got this 'fawn' move. It's all about stepping in, getting close, making sure everything's good, smoothing things out, and taking care of everyone. But then"—I clapped my hands for emphasis—"there's the 'anxious' step. You pull away on your tiptoes, always looking over your shoulder, waiting for the other shoe to drop."

She laughed. "That's . . . oddly accurate. One moment I'm playing the peacemaker, and the next, I'm like a cat on a hot tin roof."

"Exactly!" I grinned. "You've been doing this dance for so long that it's become second nature. But sometimes, it feels like you're dancing to two different songs at once, right?"

She sighed. "It's like I've got two left feet. I want to find my groove without constantly tripping over myself."

I leaned forward, getting more animated. "And you will! Now that we've named the dance, we can change the steps, remix the song. It's all about finding a rhythm that makes you feel good and helps you connect better with others."

She seemed more hopeful. "So, new dance moves?"

"Absolutely." I winked. "And trust me, you've got the moves. We just need to tweak the routine a bit."

This fawn-anxious thing might sound like a mouthful, but as with Clara, once you spot the patterns and recognize the dance, it becomes a lot easier to find your own rhythm and build stronger, healthier connections.

The Fawn-Avoidant Archetype

This is a hybrid of the fawn trauma response and avoidant attachment characterized by conflict avoidance and denying your own needs, leading to you often becoming a scapegoat and target for abuse in your relationships.

The fawn-avoidant archetype is a unique combination of two distinct attachment styles: avoidant attachment and the fawn trauma response. This archetype is characterized by a tendency to suppress one's own needs and desires in order to placate or appease others, as well as a desire to maintain distance and independence in relationships.

At the core of avoidant attachment is a fear of intimacy and a desire for independence. Those with avoidant attachment may struggle with feelings of vulnerability and have difficulty forming close emotional connections with others. This can lead to a tendency to distance oneself from others, both emotionally and physically, in order to maintain a sense of control and independence.

The fawn trauma response, on the other hand, is a coping mechanism that involves suppressing one's own needs and desires in order to placate or appease others. It is often triggered by experiences of abuse, trauma, or other forms of adversity, and is characterized by a lack of assertiveness and a tendency to "go along" with others in order to avoid conflict or maintain relationships.

The combination of these two attachment styles can be particularly challenging, as you may feel torn between a desire for independence and a need to please or appease others in order to maintain relationships. This can lead to a cycle of suppression and avoidance; as you struggle to assert your own needs and desires, you may have difficulty forming close, emotionally intimate connections with others.

Fawn-avoidant individuals are often hyper-focused on the moods and expectations of others. When conflict arises, they often blame themselves for not being able to make things work, covertly doubling down on efforts to win their partners back. They hate the idea of being seen as needy and instead focus on being worthy of love by twisting themselves tightly around meeting everyone else's needs but their own. However, deep down they crave connection. When their relationships require too much vulnerability, they pull away at the first sign of abandonment or affections not being reciprocated in an effort to avoid being hurt.

During conflict, the intermittent avoidance results in disappearing acts. This can look like ghosting for a few days or withdrawing and becoming nonresponsive for a few hours. Their flavor of avoidance on one hand can look like the silent treatment; however, they may also be unsure of what to do in order to fix things in that moment.

When they return, they will quickly shift into love-bombing and people-pleasing in an effort to bring back the honeymoon period. They'll do everything they can to avoid conflict by becoming hyper-compliant in order to make up for their behavior. This is also known as push-pull behavior, and it maintains a consistent pattern of emotional volatility and uncertainty about the relationship.

This type is also a chronic caretaker, neglecting their own needs as they focus on everyone else. In relationships, they over-function and over-give in order to secure love, affection, and attention, or to keep the peace. This anxiety about working for acceptance may also look like oversharing, then later withdrawing when feeling they've said too much.

If they aren't performing in their relationships, they're unsure of the role they play. Their entire presentation is centered around working for love and retreating once they get it. In many ways, this is an unconscious process for managing their partners. They do just enough to keep them close, but maintain enough of a distance to keep intimacy and vulnerability at bay. This means they never really allow their partners to experience their real self (a person with real emotional needs).

This type may also find themselves in financially abusive and other transactional relationships, because they're often performing in exchange for potential benefits. They over-give for acceptance, love, or attention, and they may receive, for example, money, housing, or other transactional benefits.

Despite these challenges, it is important to remember that everyone has the capacity to change and grow with the right support and guidance. In the laid-back atmosphere of my office, with its chill vibes and light background music, I kicked off my shoes and pulled my feet up onto the chair, thinking about Jake's story—a classic fawn-avoidant saga.

"Alright, Jake," I began, with a playful smirk. "Let's imagine your emotional world as . . . hmm, think of it like a game of dodgeball."

He chuckled, leaning in, clearly intrigued. "Dodgeball? Seriously? Okay, hit me."

I grinned. "See, you've got this 'fawn' side of you, right? It's like you're trying to catch every ball, make sure you're in the game, always on the lookout for potential throws. But then, the 'avoidant' side steps in, and instead of catching, you're ducking, diving, and dodging away."

Jake laughed out loud. "Man, it's like you've watched me

at a company picnic! One minute I'm all in, and the next, I'm finding the nearest exit."

I snapped my fingers, pointing at him. "Bingo! It's like you're playing defense and offense at the same time. Sometimes you're the MVP, and other times you just want to sit on the sidelines."

He nodded, a reflective look in his eyes. "I wish I could just . . . I don't know, find a balance between the two?"

I stretched out, hands behind my head. "That's where the magic happens. Imagine mixing up the game—a bit of catch, a bit of dodge, but on your terms. Maybe it's about teaming up with someone, like a therapist, who knows the game inside out. Or learning some new moves, better strategies, or even just pumping yourself up with some self-love pep talks."

Jake seemed thoughtful. "So, a dodgeball remix?"

I winked. "Exactly. And who knows? With a bit of practice, you might just become the dodgeball champ with a heart of gold."

Navigating the fawn-avoidant maze can feel like a whirlwind, but once you know the rules and get the hang of the game, it's all about making it work for you, playing at your own pace, and building those winning connections.

The Flight-Avoidant Archetype

In my relaxed office corner, the mellow glow of the afternoon sun peeking in, I sank into my plush chair, thinking about Alex's story—the epitome of the flight-avoidant journey.

"Alright, picture this," I started, stretching my arms as if framing a movie scene. "You're like a world-class tightrope walker."

Alex chuckled. "You and your analogies! Go on . . ."

"You're up high, balancing with expert precision," I went on. "On one side, there's this wide-open space—freedom, control, independence. It's exhilarating. But then, on the other side, there's the crowd below, cheering for you, wanting to connect, to be closer. And that's where the wobble starts."

His eyes widened, the realization dawning. "It's like I want to soar, to be free, but any slight tug toward connection . . . and I feel like I'm falling."

"Exactly!" I said, snapping my fingers. "The flight-avoidant in you wants to sprint across that rope, feeling the wind, the rush. But there's also this nagging voice that says you've got to be perfect while doing it. No wobbles allowed. And if someone shouts from below, 'Hey, can we chat?' it feels like a gust of wind threatening to knock you off."

He nodded. "I want to be close, but it feels . . . overwhelming. So, I retreat, bury myself in work or just . . . shut down."

I leaned in. "And that's where the paradox lies. There's this part of you that wishes someone just 'got you,' that they'd magically know what you're feeling. Yet, speaking up about those emotions feels like a vulnerability, like showing a weakness."

Alex sighed. "I wish I didn't feel I had to be perfect to be loved."

"Hey," I responded gently, "no one's asking for perfection. And while the tightrope might feel precarious, remember you've got a safety net below. It's about finding your rhythm, allowing yourself to wobble, and reaching out when you need support."

He smiled softly. "So, more balance, less sprinting?"

"You got it," I said. "And trust me, the view's pretty amazing when you take a moment to enjoy it."

The flight-avoidant journey might feel like a balancing act, but with the right mindset, some self-compassion, and a pinch of bravery, it's possible to find steadiness and embrace those deeper, fulfilling connections.

9

·············

Survival-Based Relationships

Tina was always vibrant, the life of the party. Friends loved her energy. On a particularly breezy evening over coffee, she raved about her new relationship with Alex. "The connection is electric," she beamed. But as the conversation steered deeper, a different story unfolded. "The sex? Unreal. But outside the bedroom? He hardly ever texts, and we rarely go on actual dates." Tina paused, looking lost in thought. "But did I mention the sex?"

That's when I realized Tina was caught in what I've termed a "survival-based relationship." Now, if you've been following along, you'll remember our earlier discussion on survival mode. Here, we're delving into the terrain where two people bring their individual survival instincts into a relationship. Imagine it like this: instead of two people creating a harmonious melody, they sometimes end up clashing cymbals.

These relationships are intense. They revolve around addressing immediate needs rather than building emotional or psychological connections. Think of it as going for a quick snack when you're hungry versus sitting down for a nourishing meal.

A distinct hallmark of these relationships? A whirlwind of passion, struggle, misunderstandings, and often, a mismatch of core values. For instance, Tina and Alex seemed magnetically drawn to each other, yet their day-to-day interactions were marked by misalignments and missed texts. When two people prioritize differently and have different life goals, the common ground becomes a tightrope walk.

Often, such dynamics are more than just a passing phase. It's like being trapped in a time loop, replaying old patterns. However, recognizing them is the first step toward a plot twist. These relationships can be useful as mirrors that reflect unresolved emotional baggage.

While every relationship has its roller-coaster moments, it's crucial to know the difference between an exhilarating ride and one that leaves you nauseated. The takeaway? It's less about the immediate highs and lows, and more about the journey. Sometimes, understanding why we're on a particular ride is the key to choosing better adventures in the future.

In this chapter, we're going to discuss the different types of survival-based relationships and what can lead to them.

THE CYCLE OF ABUSE

Survival-based relationships can often be marked by emotional abuse. Emotional abuse is a pattern of behavior that is used to control, manipulate, or degrade another person. It can take many forms, including verbal abuse, gaslighting, isolation, and controlling behaviors.

Emotional abuse often follows a predictable cycle. It typically begins with an incident of abuse, which is then followed by a period of remorse or apology. During this period, the abuser may promise to change or to seek help in order to prevent the abuse from happening again.

However, over time, the abuser may return to their old patterns of behavior. This repeating cycle can be particularly challenging for the person on the receiving end of the abuse, as it can create confusion and uncertainty, and make it difficult to know when it is safe to trust the abuser again. Survival-based relationships can be particularly susceptible to this cycle of abuse. The victim may feel that they have few other options and may be afraid to leave the relationship.

It is important to recognize that no one deserves to be abused, and that it is possible to break the cycle of abuse and build healthier, more fulfilling relationships. However, it's also key that we recognize the dynamics of abuse, and why this can be especially difficult for those who are experiencing covert emotional abuse.

Overt emotional abuse is often characterized by clear, obvious behaviors that are intended to control, manipulate, or degrade another person. Examples of this may include verbal abuse, name-calling, threats, or other forms of verbal aggression. This type of abuse is often easy to recognize and can be difficult to ignore.

Covert emotional abuse, on the other hand, is a much more subtle and insidious form of abuse. It is characterized by behaviors that are intended to undermine the victim's sense of self-worth and self-confidence, and it can be difficult to recognize or acknowledge. Examples of this may include gaslighting, isolation, controlling behaviors, or manipulation.

Covert emotional abuse can be particularly painful, as it is often subtle, leaving the victim feeling confused and uncertain. It can also be difficult to identify, as the abuser may present themselves as supportive or caring, making it difficult for the victim to recognize that they are being abused.

Here are a few examples of covertly abusive behaviors:

Fake Apologies with No Changed Behavior: An apology without changed behavior is manipulation. The abuser continues to do what they apologized for and said they would change.

Ghosting After a Disagreement: Intentionally disappearing after conflict to teach you a lesson. They return when they feel you are ready to reset the relationship and avoid addressing the real issue.

Invalidating Your Experiences of Them: "You're too sensitive" and "I can't be myself around you" are ploys to make you feel guilty about their abusive behavior.

Using Vulnerable Information Against You: Using information about your past, previous abuse, or otherwise sensitive information against you in jest or during conflict.

Moving the Goalpost: There's always something that needs to change before the relationship can move forward. This keeps you at arm's length as you walk on eggshells toward a nonexistent goal.

Pulling Away: Using the silent treatment. This is different from withdrawing to take space to calm down, refocus, or think things through. Instead, this is an attempt to control you and the relationship by withdrawing attention, affection, and love to make you worry about being abandoned or rejected (so that they will be able to maintain or regain control).

Signs You Are Experiencing Covert Emotional Abuse

When things don't feel quite right in a relationship, and you can't put a finger on it, chances are you might be dealing with some covert emotional abuse. Here's how it can manifest:

- **Loss of Self:** You're a shell of who you used to be because their behavior chips away at your self-esteem.
- **Self-Neglect:** You stopped taking care of your emotional or physical needs.
- **Self-Harm:** You've entertained suicidal thoughts when in high conflict with them.

Now, let's break down abuse in general. Often, when you're dealing with someone who's covertly abusive, they may show tendencies of one or more of these abusive behaviors.

- **Abuse:** When someone harms or exploits you in some way. Here's the breakdown:
  - **Physical:** Direct harm to your body, like hitting or shoving.
  - **Emotional:** Messing with your feelings—constant criticism, belittling, or manipulation.

- **Mental:** Mind games, including gaslighting or making you doubt your own reality.
- **Sexual:** Any unwanted actions that invade your boundaries or personal space.

And here's where it gets really tricky; some who engage in these behaviors do so covertly and often fly under the radar:

Denial in Order to Maintain Control: They refuse to go to therapy or address the issues in your relationship.

Manipulation: They promise to change but continue to behave the same.

Control: They try to isolate you from friends or family, and control who you see and where you go.

Chaotic Behavior: You're often researching their behavior online and talking to your friends about it obsessively (meanwhile, a trauma bond is forming).

Gaslighting: Gaslighting is a form of emotional abuse in which a person manipulates someone else into questioning their own reality or sanity. This can be done through various tactics, such as denying or trivializing the other person's experiences, feelings, or perceptions, or by using selective facts or lies to distort the truth.

Now, diving deeper into the psyche, one personality type that might be at the center of such covert emotional abuse is the covert narcissist.

Covert Narcissism

You'd think narcissists would be easy to spot with their obviously arrogant behavior, right? Not the covert ones. They're sneakier, often appearing shy or playing the victim card. Their main traits are a laser focus on their own needs and a stark lack of empathy. So while they may seem vulnerable or reserved, underneath that facade might be a world of manipulation and self-centeredness. It's these very individuals, the covert narcissists, who can be master puppeteers in the realm of emotional abuse.

Covert narcissism is a type of narcissism that is characterized by a focus on one's own emotional needs and a lack of empathy for others. It is often difficult to recognize, as covert narcissists may present themselves as shy, vulnerable, or humble, making it easy for them to fly under the radar and avoid detection.

One of the key characteristics of covert narcissism is a deep-seated sense of insecurity and a need for constant validation. As a result, covert narcissists may rely on others to boost their ego and validate their worth. They may also engage in manipulative or controlling behaviors in order to get their own way or maintain a sense of control.

Despite their need for validation, covert narcissists often struggle with empathy and may have a hard time understanding or caring about the feelings of others. This can make it difficult for them to form close, emotionally intimate relationships, and can leave their partners feeling unvalued and unsupported. Here are some common characteristics and behaviors to look out for:

Temperament: Initially presents with an even temperament and carefully curated image, which later unravels as resentment builds due to internal conflict when they are challenged or rejected.

Curated Image: Chooses partners or friends based on superficial characteristics like age, intelligence, weight, reputation, perceived dominance, inferiority, and/or success.

Passive Aggression: Engages in passive-aggressive behavior, then accuses everyone else of being the problem while denying there's an issue (because they are the problem).

Low Ego Strength: Sensitive to even the slightest criticism and holds grudges due to fragile ego and low self-esteem.

False Self: Creates fantasies or stories of who they are in order to create a perception of superiority in contrast to their targets.

Self-Victimization: Always the victim, and uses that to garner sympathy. Later, they may use that sympathy to manipulate you.

Unreliable: Exhibits a lack of reliability around the things that don't benefit them or take attention away from them: known to create drama around holidays/important events, disappears when you're sick, won't show up when they say they will (in order to stir conflict and get attention, even if it's negative).

Engaging in just one of these behaviors doesn't make someone a covert narcissist. Context and patterns are important. The most common ways that covert narcissists punish their targets include gaslighting, blame shifting, stonewalling, silent treatment, passive aggression, splitting, triangulation, and manipulation.

The problem with this type of person is that they aren't readily identifiable early on; they're very invested in presenting themselves as "nice." However, if you're paying attention, you'll start to see the discrepancies between who they say they are and who they truly know themselves to be. For this reason, they also struggle with debilitating anxiety around how they're perceived and consequentially enmesh themselves with friends, partners, or business associates in order to create an extension of themselves. If they choose a partner who is successful, it means they will be perceived as successful. This is how they build the illusion to their peers or social group.

Covert narcissists typically gravitate toward people with fragile emotional boundaries. Those who run around saying, "They chose me because of my light," are often painfully incorrect. It's not merely your kindness or your light that draws them in. Often, it's an unresolved trauma bond that you unintentionally symbolize for them. Their choice of a partner revolves around what benefits them directly. The crucial thing is discerning whether their actions cultivate a space that lacks safety and clarity.

Avoid trying to armchair-diagnose and focus instead on what makes you want to stay in order to save, change, or fix them.

THE PREMATURE ATTACHMENT RELATIONSHIP

Covert narcissism, with its subtle manipulations and need for validation, is indeed a function of codependency, revealing just how layered and complex our patterns of connection can be. As we delve deeper into this terrain, we uncover another facet of codependency that warrants our attention: premature attachment. This particular pattern, while distinct in its manifestations, shares the same fertile ground of neglecting one's own needs in favor of external validation—a theme that resonates profoundly with the nature of codependent relationships. By unraveling these threads, we aim to shed light on how these dynamics interact, influence one another, and ultimately shape our journey toward genuine connection and self-awareness.

When we speak of codependency, we are referring to a relational pattern in which one's sense of worth and well-being is intricately tied to the behavior and state of another. It's a form of over-investment in another person's world, often leading to the neglect of one's own feelings, needs, and overall well-being. In the depths of codependency, it's not uncommon to see feelings of worthlessness, inadequacy, and low self-esteem taking root as you lose yourself in the quest to please and care for others.

In this intricate dance, the ego often steps in as a form of protection, creating a false sense of security and helping to shield you from further hurt and pain. However, this protective mechanism can also serve to perpetuate the cycle of codependency, as it keeps you locked in patterns of neglecting yourself and seeking validation from others.

Now, let's go deeper into the concept of premature attachment, a phenomenon that finds its place under the broad umbrella of codependency. Premature attachment speaks to the haste in forming deep connections before a solid foundation of trust and understanding has been established. It's a rush toward intimacy, fueled by a desire to escape old wounds, feelings of abandonment, and a deep-seated fear of rejection.

This premature leap into connection is intrinsically connected to codependency. It stems from the same root of seeking validation and worth from others, of turning outward for reassurance rather than cultivating it within. In the whirlwind of premature attachment, we often find ourselves neglecting our own needs, bypassing the process of truly getting to know the other person, and diving headlong into a connection that may not serve our well-being.

In practice, these patterns of codependency and premature attachment play out in various ways. Sometimes, we may find ourselves in relationships where our needs are sidelined. Other times, this can look like jumping from one intense connection to another, seeking stability in the arms of others but never quite finding it.

Addressing these patterns requires a gentle unraveling, a turning inward to understand the roots of these behaviors. It means learning to cultivate a sense of worth and stability from within, creating a balance between connection with others and a deep, abiding connection with oneself.

By integrating the concept of codependency into the discussion of premature attachment, we now see the interconnected-ness of these patterns, providing a clearer picture of the dynamics at play. It's an invitation to heal, to transform these patterns of connection, and to create relationships that are rooted in balance, self-respect, and genuine connection.

Here's what we can do:

Reconnect with Ourselves: This isn't just about today. It's about every version of us, especially the younger ones with dreams and scars.

Practice Regular Self-Care: This is about more than spa days. It's about acknowledging our worth every single day.

Face Our Past: Ignoring old wounds won't make them disappear. Recognizing them is the first step toward healing.

Be There for Our Inner Child: That younger self, with their dreams, fears, and hopes, needs to know the present you has got their back.

By focusing on these, we set the foundation for healthier, more genuine connections in the future. As we continue our journey through the landscape of survival-based relationships, next up is the realm of obsessive and romanticized relationships.

The Obsessive, Fantasized, Romanticized Relationship

The obsessive, fantasized relationship can be a maze of emotions. We get so entangled in the allure of what could be that we lose sight of what truly is. Those deep dives into daydreams where every interaction gets magnified, every moment replayed with added flair—it's a testament to our mind's incredible ability to paint vivid pictures.

But, you know, it's interesting how our minds work. We meet someone, and before we know it, we've crafted this detailed story about who they are, based on tidbits of information and our own hopes. When the real person doesn't align with that carefully constructed narrative, it feels off-putting. It's almost as if they didn't stick to the script we wrote for them. But here's the thing: often, this internal script-writing says more about our own perceptions and desires than about the true essence of the other person.

When this happens, it's indicative of a deeper pattern: you might be more committed to the stories in your mind than to the tangible reality you're experiencing. If you've faced relational trauma, there's a tendency to detach from personal emotional needs and use fantasies as a coping mechanism. Picture it like this: amid past pain or challenges, you might have dreamed of a knight in shining armor or another protective figure. Now, in present relationships, you're superimposing those age-old fantasies onto your current partner.

The curious and often challenging part is how our unconscious mind operates. It's always working, always processing, and here's the kicker: it's always trying to heal you. Your unconscious mind attempts to create scenarios or attractions to individuals that remind you of your past traumas. It's as if it's nudging you and saying, "Hey, remember this unresolved issue? Let's face it now." The aim is wholeness, completeness. It wants to close those old chapters by bringing them to the forefront, urging you to confront and heal.

But there's a catch. If you don't recognize this unconscious instinct, you can get stuck in a loop, repeating history with various partners. When you're operating from this disconnected space, the pain multiplies. My client Kathy knew this disappointment all too well.

I arrived at my office early to prepare for my first client of the day. The sun was shining through the window, casting a warm glow on my desk. I took a deep breath and centered myself, ready to help my client navigate their inner world.

As the clock struck 9 A.M., my client, Kathy, walked into the room. She had a nervous energy about her, fidgeting with her hands and avoiding eye contact.

"Good morning, Kathy. How are you feeling today?" I asked.

"I'm feeling okay, I guess," she replied, still looking away.

"Is there something specific you'd like to talk about today?" I prodded gently. Kathy took a deep breath and began to open up about her new love interest.

She described how they had met and how she felt an instant connection. She talked about how she couldn't stop thinking about them. Even though they had only been on a few dates, she had already started to plan out their future together.

"I just feel like they're the one for me," she said with a dreamy look in her eyes.

I listened intently as she continued to describe her infatuation. It was clear that she was completely smitten and had romanticized this person to the point where she didn't really know who they were.

"Kathy, it sounds like you're really caught up in the fantasy of this person and the future you've created in your mind," I said gently. "But have you taken the time to really get to know them and understand who they are as a person?"

Kathy's face sank. "No, I haven't. I guess I've just been so caught up in my own head that I haven't really paid attention to who they actually are."

I could see the disappointment and sadness in her eyes. "It's okay, Kathy. This is a common pattern when we become infatuated with someone. We create an idealized version of them in our minds and don't always see them for who they truly are."

As we continued to talk about her feelings, I helped Kathy realize that it was important to slow down and take the time to really get to know this person before making any big decisions about the future. I also encouraged her to explore her own inner world and work on building her self-esteem and self-worth, so that she didn't feel the need to rely on someone else to complete her. The path forward is reconnection with the self. It's about tuning into the genuine needs and core values we touched on in Part 1: consistency, certainty, clarity, commitment, communication, safety, and security.

By recognizing and prioritizing these needs, Kathy could ground herself in reality. This provides a foundation to choose partners who genuinely cater to these aspects, rather than getting lost in a mirage of fantasies. And ultimately, it paves the way for healthier, more fulfilling relationships.

Over the next few weeks, Kathy began to shift her focus from her love interest to her own personal growth. She started working on building her self-esteem through journaling and self-care practices. She also took the time to get to know her love interest on a deeper level and realized that they were not the perfect person she had imagined them to be, but that was okay. She was learning to love and accept them for who they truly were.

In the end, Kathy found a sense of peace and contentment within herself. She no longer felt the need to obsess over her love interest or plan out their future together. Instead, she was focused on living in the present moment and enjoying the journey, wherever it might lead.

The Fixer Relationship

In fixer relationships, we often become captivated by someone's "potential," almost like we've found a personal DIY project. But potential shouldn't be the only metric for choosing a partner. In fact, focusing solely on potential can make us overlook the true essence of a person. It's like we become entranced by the blueprint without acknowledging that the foundation might be shaky. The other person paints a picture of commitment using only the colors of potential, leaving us hoping for more, yet often receiving less.

For instance, they talk about their dream job but rarely make an effort to apply. And rather than standing back, you find yourself sending out applications on their behalf. They give mixed signals about wanting a relationship while doing all the couple-y things with you. All the while, you're weaving tales of a future where they finally, wholeheartedly, choose you. Sound familiar?

This tendency to be attracted to "potential" often stems from a lack of self-worth. It's almost as if by helping someone reach their potential, we validate our own worthiness. Consider this: Can a relationship truly flourish if you view your partner as someone to be "fixed" rather than as an equal? For genuine connections, both partners need to be on equal footing. It's essential to be with someone for who they are now, not just for who they might become.

Now, this isn't to say we should only date those who've "made it." Everyone is on their own journey. But it's vital that we choose a partner who is actively moving, growing, and striving toward their goals.

At the heart of every "fixer" lies a deep-seated belief: "If I can just make them better, it means I'm worthy." This belief often isn't about the person they're trying to "fix" at all, but a reflection of their own feelings of inadequacy. An inclination to control or "fix" someone frequently stems from our own self-abandonment, prioritizing another's emotional needs over ours, often to our own detriment. It's a safety net: by choosing partners we feel we can guide or change, we shield ourselves from vulnerability. When love has always felt like a transaction—a constant giving without reciprocation—the idea of an equal partnership can be genuinely foreign and even unsettling.

But remember, perpetual mothering and micromanaging can erode genuine intimacy. In doing so, you might be inadvertently setting yourself up as a caregiver, rather than as an equal partner.

Think of Sarah. Sarah spent her childhood playing peacekeeper between her constantly bickering parents. She became the glue trying to hold everything together, believing that if she just tried hard enough, she could make everything right. As she grew older, this became her relationship blueprint. She met Alex, a talented musician who often spoke of big dreams but rarely took actionable steps toward them. Sarah stepped in, believing that with her guidance and support, he would soar. But over time, it became clear: she was pouring her energy into a void, hoping that if she could "fix" Alex, it would validate her worth.

Through introspection and therapy, Sarah came to a revelation. Her compulsion to "fix" was less about Alex and more about healing the little girl inside her, the one who thought she wasn't enough unless she was mending something broken. Embracing this truth allowed Sarah to seek relationships with partners who celebrated her for who she was, not just what she could do for them.

For all the "fixers" out there, understand this: your worth is not contingent on your ability to repair someone else. You deserve love that sees and values you without conditions or expectations. A partnership should be a dance of two whole people, not a project. Recognize your patterns, honor your feelings, and give yourself the love you've so freely given to others. Your heart, after all, deserves its own kind of "fixing"—one that leads to true fulfillment and peace.

The Trauma-Bonded Relationship

Trauma bonding is more than a tangled relationship dynamic; it's a reflection of wounds that often date back to childhood. Imagine being pulled into a love that promises warmth, only to be met with coldness soon after. The roller coaster of highs and lows becomes your definition of love, but it's far from healthy.

Childhood forms the bedrock of our emotional world. When that foundation is marked with abuse or neglect, it fractures our perception of love. As children, we seek understanding in chaos. Faced with hurt from those meant to care for us, we often wrongly conclude, "It's my fault." This misbelief tragically intertwines love with pain.

Flash forward to adulthood, and the scars remain, often unnoticed on the outside. Those early emotional wounds now play out in our relationships. The toxic shame and emotional wounds from our past don't just linger; they mold our choices, steering us toward similar pain.

When adults with these wounds seek love, they unknowingly step into familiar territories of rejection and hurt. They might believe they're simply "loving deeply," but this intensity is an echo of past traumas. Chasing someone who continuously rejects you isn't passion; it's an old wound screaming for attention.

That inner critic whispering, "You're not good enough," is an echo of the past, likely shaped by caregivers who were overly critical or absent. In these entangled relationships, moments of kindness from the abuser become like a balm, momentarily soothing the hurt. But with each cycle, the pain digs deeper, strengthening the bond of trauma.

The Love-Addicted Relationship

Let's unpack the cycle that ensnares us in the same types of toxic relationships time and again. Each time the initial thrill with a new partner starts to wane, there's an inner impulse driving you toward drama. This isn't merely about craving chaos; it's about chasing the intoxicating "high" that marked the early days of the relationship. The result? An emotional roller coaster where you're constantly yearning for the peaks, even if they're interspersed with harrowing lows.

The science behind this is intriguing. Being drawn to challenging partners leads to spikes in hormones like adrenaline and norepinephrine. When combined with the body's natural opiates, it results in that overwhelming feeling of infatuation. In simple terms, the more challenging the partner, the more intense the emotional response.

The human brain seeks comfort in what's familiar. If the familiarity you've known is chaos and volatility, then that becomes your brain's comfort zone. It's a tough cycle to break, especially when every cell in your body is wired for attachment, even if that attachment is to unpredictability.

THE PITFALLS OF OVER-PRIORITIZING EARLY SEXUAL CHEMISTRY

Sex can mean many things to us as adults, but one of its most powerful functions is the ability to connect us with the feelings we yearned for as children. This is particularly true for those of us who experienced emotional neglect in our upbringing.

For many of us, our parents were focused on survival, providing the basics like food, shelter, and clothing. While they did the best they could with the resources they had, it often meant that our emotional needs went unmet.

As a result, we learned to bury these feelings. Some of us channeled them into academic or professional success as a way to feel seen and validated. Others may have turned to relationships, searching for the love and validation they missed in childhood. What both groups have in common is the deep need for connection and a tendency to act on early sexual chemistry as a way to secure it.

We may tell ourselves that we need to "test the chemistry" before anything else, but what we're really saying is that we'd rather bypass the usual process of building a connection because we are disconnected from our own emotional needs.

To allow people to get to know who we really are, we have to be vulnerable. If we experienced emotional neglect as children, we may have learned to disconnect from our emotions. This emotional unavailability can lead us to try to meet our desire for affection and attention by seeking out and acting on sexual chemistry. We bypass the time it takes to get to know someone in an attempt to avoid vulnerability, and we settle for sex. The problem is, we seek it from people who mirror the emotionally neglectful dynamics from earlier in our lives.

Repetition compulsion drives this pattern of behavior as we try to unconsciously re-create our unresolved emotional experiences from childhood as adults. However, this often results in a growing attachment hunger, because we don't know how to cultivate true connection. After all, we weren't taught how to do so by our parents, who were themselves focused on survival.

As a result, we may continue this pattern in our adult lives, entering into transactional relationships based on sex or money.

Physical attraction alone doesn't sustain a relationship. While passion ignites the initial flame, it's intimacy that kindles it, and deep connection that maintains its glow. Nurturing this passion requires mutual vulnerability, empathy, and the courage to engage in difficult conversations about our roles in the relationship.

After that initial spark and whirlwind romance, we all quickly realize that there's so much more to a lasting relationship. Sure, that electric charge is exciting, but it's the deeper intimacy and connection that make a relationship really glow. And here's the thing: our past, especially the parts that might be tinged with childhood neglect, can play a sneaky role in how we build relationships with others now.

Imagine our childhood coping behaviors as old, worn-out tools in a toolbox. Once upon a time, they were super helpful, maybe even life-saving. But in our adult world, especially in our relationships, they might not be the right tools for the job anymore. Healing is kind of like updating that toolbox, getting rid of the tools we don't need, and adding in some shiny new ones that serve us better.

It's all about understanding our emotional history, seeing its influence, and then deciding to grow from there. And that growth? It's wrapped up in patience, self-compassion, and an unwavering commitment to being our best selves. So, as we journey on, let's aim to nurture our relationships with that same compassion and insight, building connections that are not just passionate, but also deep and truly fulfilling.

My client Tina was a great example of this. Tina, a striking woman, came into my office in a flurry of emotions. On the surface, her confidence was unmistakable, turning heads as she entered. But once she sat down, she seemed to shed that external armor, her words stumbling out between sobs. Tina was in a rough spot, facing criminal charges after a confrontation with her boyfriend. The ups and downs of their relationship were punctuated by intense physical intimacy, which Tina saw as her only way of truly connecting with him.

To understand Tina's present, we had to explore her past. Growing up, Tina's parents were all about achievements. Emotional validation? Not so much. They were too caught up in their own grind, leaving Tina feeling unseen and unheard. When disagreements erupted between her parents, Tina would often side with her father, resulting in icy silences from her mother that could last for months. This early environment lacked the kind of parental mirroring and emotional attunement crucial for a child's emotional development.

Tina's past became a prologue in her relationships. She sought out partners reminiscent of the emotional void she felt in childhood, like her current boyfriend. He lacked the ability to validate her emotions, yet she worked tirelessly to win his affection, much like how she had tried to gain her mother's attention during the silent treatments. And, ironically, when Tina encountered people who offered emotional security and validation, she found them boring.

Tina's story is a vivid example of how unresolved childhood issues can manifest in our adult relationships. Her deep-seated feelings of abandonment, rejection, and inadequacy compelled her to seek partners that felt familiar but were ultimately harmful. Our mind often seeks what it knows, even if that's not what's best for us.

There's an essential lesson in Tina's tumultuous story: recognizing and challenging the dysfunctional patterns we've grown accustomed to is the first step toward healing.

For Tina, our sessions together revolved around developing this awareness. We delved into her childhood, shedding light on the root causes of her relationship choices. Together, we discussed actionable steps she could take to disrupt these patterns:

Self-Awareness: Before making decisions, especially in relationships, take a step back and assess whether the choice is based on old patterns or genuine compatibility.

Affirmations: Reinforce your self-worth daily. Remind yourself that you deserve love, respect, and validation.

Therapeutic Support: Consider group or individual therapy to unpack childhood trauma and provide a safe space to heal and grow.

Education: Read up on attachment styles and parental mirroring to better understand and break the cycle.

Mindful Interactions: Before reacting, especially with loved ones, pause and ask: "Is this my authentic self reacting, or am I operating from old wounds?"

Set Boundaries: Recognize when to say no or walk away from situations or relationships that rekindle harmful patterns.

As our sessions progressed, Tina began to implement these strategies. She sought out healthier relationships, and over time, her interactions with her children and others started reflecting a newfound understanding and growth. While the journey of self-discovery and healing is ongoing, with the right guidance and tools one can pivot toward healthier, more fulfilling relationships. Tina's story is a testament to the strength of the human spirit and the transformative power of awareness and intention.

The Emotionally Neglected Child as a Hypervigilant, Love-Starved Adult

Childhood emotional neglect can have a lasting impact on our relationships and attachment styles in adulthood. As children, if our emotional needs are not met, we are left with feelings of emptiness and longing. This often results in the development of anxious attachment, where we become overly dependent on external sources for validation and love. Our relationships then become a way to quell the anxiety, with external connections taking priority over the connection to ourselves.

When we lack self-worth and self-esteem, we become hypervigilant and desperate for approval from others. We may go out of our way to please others, often at the cost of our own well-being, which can lead to resentment and unfulfilled needs. Our attachment style becomes centered around needing constant validation, which can result in toxic relationships.

The first step in healing from childhood emotional neglect is recognizing its impact on our lives and our attachment styles. By learning to communicate our needs, we can establish healthy boundaries with others and take ownership of our own emotions. Take Lila, for example. Lila had always been the "yes" person. Her drive to appease and be seen in a favorable light was a vestige of her childhood emotional neglect. Growing up, her emotions were like unwelcome guests: she learned early on to stifle them, presenting a facade of calm and strength even when storms raged within. As an adult, this translated into a web of codependency that manifested in every sphere of her life.

At work, Lila would often find herself buried under heaps of tasks, always saying "yes" to more work even when she felt stretched to her limit. Memories of childhood confrontations held her back from asserting herself. But with the support of a trusted colleague, Lila started practicing boundary-setting through role-playing exercises. Gradually, she learned to prioritize her mental health and well-being over external validation.

In her personal life, her default response to "How are you?" was always a rehearsed "I'm fine." This was until she decided to confront her disconnect with her emotions. Each evening, Lila took out a journal, capturing the myriad emotions that played out during the day. This simple reflection exercise allowed her to reconnect with her feelings, and to really understand and express them.

Lila's friendships were not exempt from her codependent tendencies. Getting close and being vulnerable were a challenge. Emotional vulnerability had been seen as a sign of weakness during her childhood, and these memories held her back. But Lila took small steps to change this. She began sharing personal stories with close friends, actively participating in deeper conversations, and gradually breaking down her barriers.

In Lila's relationships, particularly romantic ones, there was always an undercurrent of need for validation. Lila would seek constant reassurance, a legacy from times when parental praise was rare and always followed by a critique. To combat this pattern, she initiated a practice of self-validation. At the end of each day, she'd write down three things she did well, appreciating her own achievements rather than waiting for acknowledgment from others.

Despite everything in her life seeming to be in place, Lila often grappled with a nagging feeling of emptiness. In those times, she would resort to mindfulness exercises, like focusing on her breathing or the feel of her fingers brushing against the fabric of her couch. These grounding exercises gave her a sense of connection, a tether to the present.

As Lila began integrating these strategies into various aspects of her life, she found herself breaking free from the chains of codependency. She realized that healing wasn't a destination but a continuous journey, and with each step, she was crafting a life of genuine happiness and fulfillment.

Remember, you are not alone in this journey toward healing and understanding. You have the power to make changes in your life and create a healthy, fulfilling relationship with yourself and others. By taking the time to heal, you can find peace within yourself and live a life of true happiness and fulfillment.

Casual Sex and Unresolved Attachment Wounds

Navigating the modern dating world with underlying attachment trauma can feel like being a fish out of water. See, at the core of attachment trauma is a profound yearning for genuine connection, security, and affirmation. So when we delve into today's dating scene, which often celebrates fleeting connections and surface-level interactions, we're setting ourselves up for a challenging journey.

Think of it this way: with attachment trauma, we're already primed to seek out validation, even if it's just a crumb. Casual sex can sometimes feel like a quick fix for that hunger—a momentary "high" that says, "See, I'm wanted." But just like junk food might temporarily satiate but doesn't nourish, these short-lived encounters don't feed our deeper emotional needs.

The issue isn't with casual sex per se; it's when we use sex as an emotional band-aid. Just like in any arena, it's important to understand our motivations. If we're seeking casual encounters to genuinely explore and enjoy our sexuality, great! But if it's a mask for deeper unmet needs or unresolved trauma, we might be in for a cycle of short-term pleasure and long-term dissatisfaction.

Mixing attachment trauma with modern casual sex culture can be like trying to quench thirst with saltwater. It might feel like what we need in the moment, but it only intensifies our yearning for real connection.

Back to our food analogy: the beauty of choice is that it gives us the freedom to select what truly nourishes us, like stepping up to an endless buffet. We need to be mindful, though. With the vast array of options, it's easy to binge on what's immediately satisfying rather than what's ultimately fulfilling. While the modern dating landscape offers many avenues for connection, we need to ensure these connections resonate with our deeper desires and needs, especially if we're navigating the world with attachment wounds.

So yes, enjoy the thrill and spontaneity of today's dating scene. But remember, in the midst of all the swiping and fleeting encounters, it's okay to pause and ask: "Is this truly what I want? Does it align with my deeper needs?" Because while casual can be fun, connection is what truly satisfies the soul.

The Addiction to Volatility

In today's fast-paced world of swipes and likes, the lines between genuine connection and fleeting moments can blur. Sometimes we chase the highs of casual encounters, mistaking them for the deep intimacy we truly crave. It's like grabbing a candy bar when your soul is yearning for a wholesome meal. But other times, in the midst of all this, we might find ourselves drawn to relationships that mimic the ups and downs of a roller coaster. Why is that? Well, it's because there's a deeper layer underneath—the addiction to volatility.

Let's gently peel back the layers and truly understand what's going on inside. We are creatures of habit. Our behaviors, thoughts, and emotions are sculpted through repeated experiences, forging neural pathways that determine how we react to situations, especially in relationships. Often, these patterns originate in our past, specifically from those volatile relationships that gave us an emotional high. We can end up craving them like an adrenaline junkie thirsts for the next big thrill.

Take, for instance, the fascinating work of Susan Anderson in *The Journey from Abandonment to Healing*. She touches upon the chemical allure behind our emotions. According to Anderson, being with someone challenging gives our system a rush of catecholamines—neurochemicals like adrenaline and norepinephrine. This biochemical cocktail, mingling with our body's natural opiates and other hormones, stirs up infatuation: a potent, euphoric feeling that makes intimacy seem effortless, even with someone we've just met.

It's intoxicating, really. When this intoxication is coupled with someone who's emotionally unavailable, it keeps the biochemical thrill alive. But when someone comes into our lives who's emotionally present and committed, the rush wanes. Suddenly, the chemistry seems to be missing, replaced by an unnerving stillness that can drive us away in search of another emotional high.

This cyclical search for the "high" can also mean that when a new partner doesn't stimulate that same rush, we might subconsciously incite drama, chaos, and uncertainty to recapture that addictive emotional roller coaster. Why? Because our brains are remarkably attuned to seeking attachment and safety in what we know, even if that familiarity is steeped in chaos and volatility.

Yet, the real challenge (and solution) lies in recognizing and breaking this cycle. It's about acknowledging that genuine connection doesn't stem from unrest and uncertainty. True intimacy is built on trust, understanding, and stability.

In essence, breaking free from the addiction to volatility is an empowering journey of self-awareness, patience, and deliberate action. It's about choosing peace over chaos and genuine connection over fleeting highs.

Navigating relationships can be tricky, especially when you add past traumas to the mix. Our ego tries to protect us from getting hurt again, while our inner self is hiding away all those tough emotions. It's kind of like walking a tightrope, trying to balance who we really are with the version of ourselves we show to the world.

Now, throw modern dating into the equation—with its quick

swipes and temporary connections—and things get even trickier. For those of us dealing with attachment issues, it's not as simple as a right swipe. We find ourselves questioning every connection: "Is this just a way to pass the time, or is it something real?" And just when we think we have it all figured out, we find ourselves drawn back to those unpredictable, up-and-down relationships.

But here's the good news: there's light at the end of the tunnel. By putting in the work to heal our hearts, practicing mindfulness, setting clear boundaries, and reaching out for support, we can find our way back to ourselves. These practices are like having a roadmap in the complicated world of relationships, reminding us to stop, think, and move forward with purpose. With the right tools and a bit of patience, we can navigate through it all and find meaningful connections.

BREAKING THE CYCLE

James grew up in an unpredictable emotional climate. His father was a puzzle, a force James could never truly decipher. One moment, his father would be warm and inviting, drawing James into a hug or a rare tender conversation. But in the blink of an eye, the warmth would vanish, replaced by a coldness that felt like a winter gust. James became all too familiar with this icy aloofness, even starting to expect it.

This emotional dance was exhausting. As a child, James learned to tread lightly, attempting to predict his father's moods, trying to be the perfect son to keep the warmth lasting just a bit longer. Every cold phase instilled a quiet desperation in James, an anxiety to "fix" things so he could return to the fleeting moments of warmth.

Fast-forward to James's adult life. The women he found himself attracted to had an eerily familiar pattern of warmth followed by withdrawal. These relationships felt like home, but not in a comforting sense. They echoed the unpredictable love he had known as a child. He became a pursuer, constantly trying to reclaim the affection that would inevitably wane. More often than not, this chase led to heartbreak, reinforcing his childhood belief that love was something elusive, to be earned and fought for.

The turning point came during a therapy session. As James recounted a recent relationship's highs and lows, his therapist drew a parallel between this relationship and his dynamic with his father. The patterns matched: the pursuit, the anxiety, the constant yearning for validation.

With therapy, James began to peel back the layers of his emotional wounds. He confronted the young boy within him who so desperately sought his father's consistent love. Through introspection, he began to understand that his attraction to unpredictable love wasn't a masochistic choice, but rather a subconscious attempt to "right the wrongs" of his childhood.

He delved into self-compassion, learning to extend the love he so freely gave others to himself. And with time, James's definition of love evolved. No longer was it an unpredictable force. He sought, and found, a relationship built on consistent warmth, understanding, and mutual respect. A relationship where love wasn't a puzzle to solve, but a comforting embrace to come home to.

**REFLECTION EXERCISE: BREAKING THE
ADDICTION TO VOLATILE RELATIONSHIPS**

As you consider how toxic shame shows up in your life, pause
and take a moment to think about any remnants of toxic
shame lingering around in your heart and mind.

STEP 1   What are some of the issues that hold an emotional
           trigger for you because of the pain it roots when it comes
           into your awareness? Make a list.

STEP 2   Pause and pay specific attention to the physiological
           responses that come up for you.

STEP 3   Make a list of where toxic shame shows up and how the
           decisions you make and things you tolerate or avoid stem
           from it.

STEP 4   Journal about what comes up for you as well as the
           automatic negative thoughts that fuel the shame for you.

STEP 5   Self-soothe as you take the time to focus on this area of
           your life. You'll have unexpected feelings that come up
           and it's best to sit with these, breathing through them
           while recognizing they will and allowing them to pass.

STEP 6   When you feel safe, make a list of the necessary changes
           you need to make.

REFLECTIONS

- What is an earlier event in life that fuels toxic shame for
  you?
- In what ways does this memory influence the relationship you have with yourself?
- What negative thoughts come up when you make a
  mistake, a relationship fails, or you feel abandoned/
  rejected?

Lurking negative core wounds and beliefs can show up in the following ways:

People Pleasing: Consider the shame you feel when you want to stand up for your needs but back down. Pay attention to the emotions that come up in that moment between the event or request and your response. Is it possible that toxic shame determines whether you'll acquiesce or speak up?

Situationships: In thinking about regrettable relationships, what decisions were driven by the shame you felt that compelled you to move forward against your own boundaries, standards, and deal breakers? If you never wanted to be in that situationship, consider the following to help you understand why you may have accepted it or stayed:

- **Seeking Validation:** We enter or remain in situationships due to a desire for validation and acceptance, even if the relationship isn't fulfilling our needs. The ambiguity of the situationship can create a space where we are constantly seeking reassurance and proof of our worth from the other person.
  * Negative Core Wounds: This need for validation can be traced back to negative core wounds that have left us feeling unworthy or not good enough. The situationship becomes a ground for replaying these old patterns, as we look to others to fill the void left by unhealed wounds.

- **Fear of Abandonment:** The lack of clarity and commitment in a situationship can trigger intense fears of abandonment, as we're left uncertain about where we stand in the relationship.
  * Negative Core Wounds: These fears often stem from early experiences of abandonment or instability, leading to a deep-seated belief that we're not worth committing to or staying for. The situationship perpetuates this fear, as the lack of commitment mirrors these old beliefs.
- **Tolerance of Ambiguity and Disrespect:** In situationships, we may tolerate ambiguity, inconsistency, and even disrespect, often rationalizing the behavior or making excuses for the other person.
  * Negative Core Wounds: This tolerance can be linked to negative core wounds that taught us to accept less than we deserve, reinforcing feelings around unworthiness and inadequacy.
- **Difficulty in Setting Boundaries:** The undefined nature of situationships can make it challenging to set and maintain clear boundaries.
  * Negative Core Wounds: This difficulty may be rooted in negative core wounds related to neglect or disrespect of our needs and boundaries in early life, leading to patterns around not being able to stand up for ourselves because we haven't owned our self-worth.

- **Impact on Self-Esteem:** Prolonged involvement in a situationship can take a toll on our self-esteem, as the lack of commitment and clarity can leave us questioning our worth and desirability.
  * Negative Core Wounds: This impact on self-esteem echoes the negative core wounds, further ingraining beliefs that we're not enough or aren't worthy of a committed, respectful relationship.
- **Obsessive Thoughts:** Obsessive thoughts in this context are largely about avoidance. Instead of facing the problem head-on, we loop around how to fix the situation, thinking about "woulda, shoulda, coulda," and fantasizing and romanticizing in an effort to overwrite reality—all in an effort to avoid the emotional pain that toxic shame creates.

Part III

THRIVING

10
· · · · · · · · · ·

Moving from Red Flags to Green Flags

A s we gear up to embark on Part 3 of our journey together, let's take a moment to reflect on the ground we've covered and set the stage for the exciting explorations ahead.

In Part 1, "Healing," we delved deep into the transformative process of healing. We navigated the intricacies around deciding to heal, committing to the journey, and making a bold declaration to change. We embraced the solitude of hermit mode, unpacked the Pandora's box of our past, and started the inner work necessary to grow. We also learned the importance of setting boundaries, standards, and deal breakers, and explored the various signs that point toward healing. Throughout, we focused on both internal and external aspects of healing, aiming to strike a balance that promotes genuine and lasting change.

In Part 2, "Unlocking the Pattern," we continued our exploration by examining the role of ego defense mechanisms, the unconscious mind, and the sources of toxic shame that play a critical role in our lives. We connected the dots between attachment styles, trauma responses, and the patterns of abuse that can emerge in relationships, shedding light on covertly abusive behaviors and the nuances of covert narcissism. We also tackled the complexities of premature attachment, fixer relationships, and trauma bonding, offering reflections on how lurking negative core wounds can manifest in our lives and relationships.

Now, as we stand on the cusp of Part 3, "Thriving," we are ready to take all that we have learned and apply it to forging a life filled with growth, resilience, and conscious love. We will delve into the differences between fixed and growth mindsets, unravel the power of resilience, and learn how to navigate emotional turbulence with grace. We will embrace vulnerability as a strength, explore the three pillars of conscious love, and understand what it truly means to be reborn into the best version of ourselves.

Part 3 is about more than just surviving; it's about thriving. It's about channeling the lessons from our past and the strength from our healing journey into a life that is rich, full, and utterly filled with the kind of love we've always needed from ourselves and others. Let's dive in, with hearts open and minds ready, to discover what it means to truly thrive.

It's important to remember that just like anything else worth having in life, achieving a successful conscious love relationship requires work from both parties involved. It takes effort—from being vulnerable with one another to actively practicing the skills necessary for cultivating mutual respect—to make sure that your relationship can continue growing stronger over time. It's essential to be patient with yourself (as well as your partner) during the process. After all, no two people have the same experiences or perspectives on life. We all mess up, but there are some crucial green flags to look for that help indicate someone is willing to put in the time and effort conscious love takes.

If you're looking for a relationship that is fulfilling and empowering, these green flags can help guide you to a conscious love relationship where you both can be your true selves, feel safe, and grow together. These green flags are also elements we should strive to embody ourselves.

Green flags don't mean your relationship will be perfect, but they can lead you to a more stable and fulfilling future with your partner. They signify a safe place to work through the issues that will naturally arise along the way. You'll have the tools to work through conflict instead of resorting to harmful behaviors that seek to control rather than resolve. Green flags give you the information you need about what might stand between you and feeling worthy of having a healthy and safe relationship.

For example, if trust, honesty, and open communication are important to us, then we should embody these qualities in our own behavior. This means being transparent, speaking our truth, and holding ourselves accountable for our actions. When we embody these green flags, our partners are more likely to respond in kind and treat us with the same respect and honesty we show them.

In the context of healing after toxic dynamics, the following green flags can be especially meaningful as they serve as markers of growth and progress:

Honest and Respectful Communication: Partners feel comfortable sharing their thoughts and feelings without fear of judgment or backlash. For example, having difficult conversations without invalidating each other's feelings.

Healthy Boundaries: Partners respect each other's boundaries without requiring self-abandonment. Partners who respect each other's boundaries and have open communication about their individual needs are likely to have a healthier and happier relationship.

Emotional Safety: Partners feel safe and secure in expressing their emotions, and are able to handle disagreements and conflicts in a respectful and non-toxic manner. Both parties also regulate their emotions and self-soothe to allow for clear communication without volatile or harmful behavior.

Mutual Respect: Partners view each other as equals and are committed to treating each other with dignity and kindness.

Prioritizing Emotional Growth: Partners are committed to self-improvement and supporting each other in their personal growth journeys. They acknowledge that their partner isn't supposed to meet all of their needs in the way that a parent meets the needs of a child.

Normalizing Disappointment: Partners recognize that disappointment is normal, while also guarding against resentment.

Collaborative Problem Solving: Partners work together to find solutions to challenges, rather than blaming or attacking each other.

Emotional Intimacy: Partners are able to connect on a deep, emotional level and feel comfortable being vulnerable with each other. Partners who are emotionally intimate can communicate their needs and feelings effectively, are comfortable sharing vulnerable parts of

themselves with their partner, and make an effort to
understand their partner's emotional needs.

Introspection: Partners are introspective about their own
childhood and how it impacts their relationships today.

Flexibility and Adaptability: Partners are able to adapt
and grow, while also maintaining the health and stability of their relationship.

Shared Values and Goals: Partners have similar life perspectives and aspirations that align with each other's
vision for their future.

Trust and Dependability: Partners trust each other and
feel confident in their ability to rely on each other in
times of need.

Fun and Playfulness: Partners prioritize having fun and
enjoying each other's company, even in the midst of
challenging situations.

Respect for You as an Individual and Partner: Partners
respect the time each other spends with friends and
family members, or pursuing hobbies and passion projects. They value one another's happiness outside of the
relationship.

Empathy: Partners are able to empathize with each other
and understand each other's feelings. They are supportive
during difficult times and celebrate each other's successes.

Growth Mindset: Partners are committed to personal
growth and development. They are open to learning
and trying new things, and they encourage each other
to become the best version of themselves.

Active Listening: Partners actively listen to each other
without interrupting or trying to fix the other person's
problems. They show empathy and validate their partner's feelings.

Equal Distribution of Emotional Labor: Partners share
emotional labor, which refers to the invisible work that
goes into maintaining a relationship, such as remem-
bering important dates, initiating conversations, and
planning activities. When partners share this labor, it
shows a sense of equality and care for the relationship.

Gratitude and Appreciation: Partners who regularly
express gratitude and appreciation toward each other,
even for small things, are more likely to have a positive
and fulfilling relationship.

Healthy Disagreements: Partners can have disagreements
without resorting to verbal abuse or disrespect. Instead,
they engage in healthy conflict resolution and try to
understand each other's point of view.

Supportive Communication: Partners who communicate
in a supportive and non-judgmental way can help each
other through tough times and celebrate each other's
achievements.

This is not an exhaustive list of green flags, but it serves as
a guide for finding a healthy and supportive relationship after
a toxic one. Being mindful of these positive indicators helps us
make more informed choices about the health of our relationships, and take steps to nurture and strengthen them.

By accepting these green flags, we are committing to rejecting the bare minimum. But it's important to remember that the opposite of bare minimum is not perfection; it's conscious love.

An important note: embodying green flags doesn't mean being a doormat or sacrificing our own needs. It's about striking a balance, setting boundaries, and ensuring that our own needs are met in the relationship. When both partners embody green flags, it creates a supportive, loving, and positive dynamic where both can thrive.

This is a commitment to ourselves and our relationships to embody those green flags we want to see more of. It takes effort, but the results are well worth it. A happy and healthy relationship is possible, and it starts with each of us taking responsibility for our own actions and embodying the positive qualities we want to experience.

THE DIFFERENCE BETWEEN GREEN FLAGS AND CORE VALUES

As we embrace these positive behaviors in our relationships, we step right into the realm of conscious love. It's a solid, safe space where both partners can truly be themselves, grow, and find support in each other. It's straightforward, genuine, and exactly the kind of connection that makes you feel at home, no matter where you are.

Now, think about the strong foundations of this heartfelt home. Here, we're talking about core values—the really big, deeply held beliefs that guide how you both show up in the relationship, and in life in general, which we covered in Part 1. Think honesty, deep respect, genuine empathy, and a real commitment to each other. Imagine one person deeply values honesty; this creates a transparent atmosphere where trust just blossoms. Core values are like the sturdy walls and beams of our emotional home, keeping everything stable and secure, no matter what.

Additionally, we've got green flags. These moments are like the cozy throw blankets and charming photos you scatter around, making your space feel inviting and full of warmth. These lovely, joyful touches make the journey of being together just that much sweeter. Picture thoughtful gestures, quality time spent laughing together, and those heart-to-heart talks that go on into the wee hours.

Now, let's add a layer to this. Consider a core value like open and healthy communication—it's fundamental, right? It's like deciding to use the strongest, most durable materials to build your home. A green flag corresponding to this value would look like your partner actively listening when you speak, even when the topic is a tricky one. They don't brush off your concerns or make light of them; instead, they validate your feelings and work with you to find a solution. This green flag is like adding a beautiful bay window to your well-built home, creating a space filled with light and providing a view to understand each other better.

Now, let's bring it back to the heart of the matter: conscious love. This is all about both partners really leaning in, actively building and tending to this sanctuary of love and understanding. It's about being present, open, and willing to grow together.

Choosing conscious love means you're both all in, committed to keeping those walls strong with shared values, while also relishing in the joy of adding those lovely, personal touches of green flags.

It's about creating a space where both hearts have room to breathe, heal, and simply be. A space where you can find yourselves, find each other, and build a home together in the truest sense. It's a journey filled with warmth, insight, and a whole lot of love—and honestly, it's the best kind of journey there is.

RECLAIMING OUR POWER THROUGH INNER WORK

We introduced inner work in Part 2, but now let's discuss why it's so crucial in the aftermath of a toxic relationship. When you're caught in the thick of a codependent or toxic relationship, it feels like there's no way out. But we all have the power and choice to shake things up in our relationships. It's all about rolling up our sleeves, diving into the inner work, and making the changes needed to turn our connections around and be the best versions of ourselves.

Pinpointing the Negative Cycles

To kickstart this transformation, the first step is to pinpoint those negative cycles we find ourselves in. These could be patterns where we carry the emotional load for others, react with criticism or defensiveness when we feel attacked, put others' needs ahead of our own, or resort to substances to numb the hard feelings.

Becoming aware of these patterns is crucial. It's like shining a light on the shadows, helping us spot these cycles quicker in the future and making it easier to step out of them.

Understanding Our Emotional Needs

After recognizing these unhealthy patterns, the next step is to understand the emotional needs beneath them. Ask yourself: What am I really longing for here? Is it a sense of belonging, emotional support, love, respect, understanding, or maybe freedom? Identifying these core needs is a pivotal part of healing from codependency and toxic relationships. It shifts the responsibility back to ourselves, empowering us to meet our own needs through our thoughts, words, and actions rather than waiting for someone else to fill those voids.

So, in essence, reclaiming our power in relationships is all about awareness and action. It's about recognizing the patterns that hold us back, understanding our core emotional needs, and taking proactive steps to meet those needs ourselves. This journey isn't always easy, but it's worth it. After all, it leads us to healthier, more fulfilling relationships, and ultimately, a stronger, more resilient version of ourselves.

Let's take a look at a few examples of what we can do to engage the work to thrive in our relationships:

Taking Space and Giving Space

Learning to identify the right moments to take and give space is a crucial aspect of healing from codependency and toxic relationships. Taking space allows you to step back, process your emotions, and assess the situation in a clear-headed manner. This helps you maintain your sense of self and avoid getting caught up in toxic patterns driven by reactivity. Giving others space helps preserve their sense of individuality and fosters respect and understanding in the relationship.

Knowing when to take space and when to give others space requires a certain level of emotional intelligence and self-awareness. It's important to recognize the signs that indicate you need to take space, such as feeling overwhelmed, triggered, or drained, and to take action to protect yourself when these feelings come up. Similarly, it's important to be attuned to the emotional state of others and to respond appropriately.

When you are able to strike the right balance between taking and giving space, you can cultivate a healthy and fulfilling relationship. Relationships thrive when we balance prioritizing our own well-being and staying mindful of the needs of others. This builds a strong foundation for a supportive and nourishing relationship.

SITTING WITH DISCOMFORT
BEFORE REACTING

In the previous section, I mentioned reactivity. As we heal from toxic relationships and codependency, it's important to learn how to sit with our uncomfortable feelings before reacting. This is a powerful tool that can help us take back control of our lives and make positive changes.

Benefits of Being Responsive Over Reactive

Nobody wants to be the target of someone else's venting or anger, and yet, when we're feeling agitated internally, it's common to unintentionally let those emotions spill over onto our partners. This is where the journey to self-awareness becomes crucial. Asking ourselves questions like "What am I feeling right now?" and "Why am I feeling this way?" enables us to understand the roots of our emotions, helping us address our feelings before projecting them onto our partners.

By learning to respond instead of react, we're taking control of our emotional responses during interactions with others. This includes embracing practices such as being self-aware, establishing clear boundaries in the relationship, and having open, honest communication about any issues that arise. These practices are pillars that uphold the resilience of our relationships, even when we're in the midst of internal chaos.

Responding thoughtfully begins with recognizing the signs of emotional overwhelm and taking a moment for yourself to step back and reflect. This could be as simple as pausing and taking a deep breath, creating an immediate space for your body and mind to begin to settle. If the situation allows, physically removing yourself from the conversation can give you the additional clarity you need to calm those heightened emotions.

Sitting with your emotions before responding encourages a period of reflection, helping you gain clarity on what you're truly feeling and why. This pause allows you to recognize your emotional triggers in a non-judgmental way while still maintaining your boundaries. It's about understanding these triggers not as something to be ashamed of, but as signals guiding you on how to better prepare for future interactions.

Being self-aware and knowing your triggers are like having a personal roadmap to navigate your emotional world. It doesn't mean placing blame on yourself; it's about learning and preparing. You won't need to respond to every situation, and sometimes the most powerful response is giving yourself time to sit with your feelings and understand them, and then to decide the best way forward.

When you allow yourself this space, you are actively choosing to interact from a place of strength and clarity, not from a place of emotional turmoil. The practices of journaling, deep breathing, and reflecting can be invaluable tools in this process, helping you untangle your thoughts and feelings, and guiding you toward a better understanding of yourself. This journey isn't always easy, especially when healing from past toxic relationships, but learning to respond rather than react is a crucial step toward healthier relational patterns and, ultimately, toward a healthier you.

YOUR INTUITION

In Part 1 we talked about intuition, and how to get acquainted with it in the immediate aftermath of a heartbreak. Now let's go deeper, and cover how intuition can be our guide as we reenter the dating landscape with a new self-awareness and toolkit.

Intuition is an inner knowing. It is the voice of our subconscious mind that many of us find harder to be in touch with as we age and are influenced by our formative relationships. We may not always pay attention to it, but if we do, it can lead us down the right path. Our intuition speaks to us through our thoughts, emotions, physical sensations, dreams, visions, and more. Learning how to develop and strengthen our connection with our intuition can help us make decisions that are aligned with our highest self even in times of uncertainty.

It is especially important to tap into our intuition after a toxic or codependent relationship because it cultivates a self-awareness that protects us from triggers and unhealthy patterns. Knowing when something doesn't feel right can help us recognize unhealthy dynamics before they become harmful. Our intuition also helps identify what serves and nourishes us and what doesn't. Using it, we can tune into which parts of ourselves need love and attention. This is one of the first steps to true and lasting healing.

How to Check In with Your Intuition

The first step in connecting with your intuition is being still enough to hear it speak. Practicing meditation or simply taking some time each day for self-reflection are great ways to cultivate this inner stillness, which will ultimately bring you closer to understanding yourself better. It can also provide clarity on any current issues you may be struggling with in relation to healing after traumatic experiences or toxic relationships.

As with learning to respond versus react, journaling can be a helpful tool for gaining clarity on what your inner voice is trying to tell you. From a safe environment—on the page or in a quiet room—we can explore our thoughts on difficult topics, such as codependency or other unhealthy dynamics, through self-exploration and reflection.

Taking time each day for self-reflection through meditation or journaling allows us the opportunity to connect more deeply with ourselves. Developing trust within helps ensure that we are always following the path most aligned with our highest self, even during times of uncertainty. By tapping into your internal guidance system—your intuition—you will find the strength needed to navigate tough moments as you enter into new, healthy relationships.

Fear vs. Intuition and How to Tell the Difference

When it comes to relationships, figuring out the difference between fear and intuition can be really tricky, especially if you've been in some rough spots before. If past relationships have left you on edge, it's normal to find yourself feeling scared or worried, even when things are actually going okay.

Think about it this way: fear in a relationship might show up as constant worry about your partner's actions, even when there's no clear reason to be worried. It's that nagging thought in the back of your head, based on old stuff rather than what's happening right now. It's important to catch yourself when this happens and ask, "Is there really something wrong here, or is this just something I'm not used to?"

Intuition, though, that's different. It's like a quiet friend who gives you a nudge when something's off, even if everything seems alright on the outside. It's not about panic or stress; it's a calm voice that just wants the best for you. A good way to tell them apart? Pay attention to your body. Fear usually comes with a whole bunch of stress signs—your heart might start racing or you might get sweaty palms. Intuition doesn't do that; it's more about giving you a moment of pause and clarity, without all the drama.

Understanding this can make a world of difference in your relationship. It means you can be real and open with your partner, and at the same time, trust yourself to know when something's not right. By taking a moment to step back and think things through, you're giving yourself the chance to respond in a way that's good for both you and your relationship. It's okay to feel a bit scared or unsure sometimes. The key is knowing how to handle it, and making sure fear doesn't get to call the shots. Trusting yourself and being mindful of these feelings can help steer you in the right direction.

NAVIGATING EMOTIONAL TURBULENCE

Setting Boundaries in Your Relationship

Alright, so we've talked a lot about healing yourself and how important that is. Now let's chat about how setting boundaries works in a relationship. Think of boundaries like guidelines or rules that help keep things clear and fair between you and your partner. Imagine you both have this invisible bubble around you, and setting boundaries is like telling each other, "Hey, this is my space, and there are certain things I'm cool with and some things I'm not." It's about making sure neither of you feels over-whelmed or stepped on by the other's emotions or needs.

WHY SETTING BOUNDARIES IS A GAME-CHANGER

No More Guessing Games: When you've both laid out what's okay and what's not, you're not left guessing or tip-toeing around each other. It just makes everything simpler.

Your Go-To Safe Space: You create a zone where it's to-tally okay to be yourself and share what's on your mind, even the tough stuff, without worrying about being judged or dismissed.

Keeps Things Balanced: It helps make sure one of you isn't doing all the emotional heavy lifting while the other one's just chilling. It's all about balance.

When you have clear boundaries, it's way easier to spot the good stuff in your relationship, like respect, trust, and genuine care (those are your green flags right there!). It shows you're both on the same page and really value what you have together.

HERE'S THE DEAL

Green Flags Galore: Boundaries help you see all the good stuff more clearly. If your partner is respecting your space and being supportive, that's a massive green flag!

Living Your Values: It's one thing to say you value respect and honesty, but living it out? That's where boundaries come in. They help you walk the talk.

Cool, Calm, and Collected: Instead of blowing up or shutting down when things get tough, boundaries help you respond in a chill way, keeping drama to a minimum.

MAKING IT A TWO-WAY STREET

Setting boundaries isn't just about protecting yourself; it's about building a two-way street where both of you feel safe and cared for. It's like saying, "Hey, I'm here for you, and I know you're here for me too." And here's why it works:

Trust Is Built: When you're both open and honest, and you stick to your boundaries, trust skyrockets.

Nipping Problems in the Bud: Talking about the small stuff before it turns into big stuff means fewer arguments and more happy times.

Stronger Together: All of this—the trust, the honesty, and the balance—makes your relationship stronger and ready to take on whatever comes your way.

Setting boundaries is like laying down the foundation for a rock-solid relationship. It's about creating a space where both of you can be your true selves, support each other, and build something really great together.

The Power of Vulnerability

Now that we've navigated through setting up our boundaries and spotting the green flags in a relationship, it's like we've

built a safe, cozy nest—a perfect spot for opening up and letting our guard down. This is where vulnerability steps in, and
it's a game-changer!

Setting boundaries has given us a clear understanding of
where we stand, ensuring that we're on the same page as our
partners. We've also learned to recognize the green flags—those
signs that shout out loud, "Hey, this is a good, healthy relationship!" With all this in place, we've created a safe space: a nurturing environment that invites us to be our most genuine selves.

Vulnerability is all about shedding those layers of protection and showing up as we truly are, with all our imperfections, fears, and dreams. It might sound a bit intimidating at
first, but let's dive in and see how it can do wonders for our
relationships.

Deepen Your Connection: When you open up and share
your true self, it invites your partner to do the same.
This mutual exchange of authenticity deepens your
connection, creating a bond that's strong and genuine.

Build Trust: Being vulnerable is a sign of trust. It shows
that you feel safe enough to reveal your inner world,
and this acts like a trust catalyst in your relationship.

Enhance Emotional Intimacy: Vulnerability allows for
a level of emotional intimacy that's hard to achieve
otherwise. It's like opening a direct channel to your
heart, creating a space for both of you to connect on a
deeper emotional level.

Promote Healing and Understanding: When you share
your struggles and vulnerabilities, it provides an

opportunity for healing and understanding. Your partner gets to see the real you, and this understanding can
lead to a stronger, more compassionate relationship.

Encourage Authenticity: By being vulnerable, you set
the stage for authenticity. It encourages both you and
your partner to drop the facades and be real, creating a
relationship grounded in truth and openness.

Creating a Safe Haven for Authenticity

Practicing vulnerability transforms your relationship into a safe
haven where authenticity reigns. It's like saying, "This is me,
in all my glory and with all my flaws, and I trust you enough
to show you my true colors." And when both partners can do
this? That's where the magic happens, and a deep, meaningful
connection blossoms.

Vulnerability is often seen as a weakness, something that
should be avoided. But in truth, vulnerability is one of the
most powerful tools we have for deepening our connection
with others. When we practice vulnerability, we are allowing ourselves to be seen for who we truly are—our hopes and
dreams, our fears and weaknesses—and that openness creates
an environment where both parties feel safe enough to share
deeply with each other. So, as we embark on this journey of
vulnerability, let's remember the solid foundation we've built
with our boundaries and the green flags we've recognized. With
these in place, we're ready to open up, connect on a deeper
level, and create a relationship that's rich in authenticity, trust,
and love.

RESPONDING VS. REACTING

Practicing vulnerability also means practicing being intentionally responsive with the people in our lives, rather than allowing immediate emotional reactions to guide our conversations. Responding is about taking a moment to pause, reflect, and then act in a considered way. On the other hand, reacting is more immediate and emotional, often without much thought put into the consequences of our actions. In the context of relationships, embracing vulnerability means opening up about your thoughts, feelings, and needs. Honesty and openness are the building blocks of trust and intimacy. But here's the kicker—it's not just about being open; it's also about how we handle our partner's openness, and that's where responding instead of reacting comes into play. Being vulnerable through responsive conversations allows for:

Safe Space for Exploration: When your partner is being vulnerable with you, responding thoughtfully creates a safe space for exploration. It tells them, "I am here, I am listening, and your feelings matter." This is the cornerstone of a relationship where both parties feel heard and respected.

Healthy Navigation Through Differences: Vulnerability also means opening up about things that might be bothering us or areas where we feel different from our partners. Here, responding instead of reacting is crucial. By taking the time to understand, reflect, and then communicate, we ensure that these moments of honesty lead to greater understanding and healthy navigation through differences, rather than misunderstandings or conflict.

Cultivating Deeper Connection: The ultimate goal of being vulnerable and responding thoughtfully is to foster a deep, meaningful connection. When we know that our vulnerability will be met with understanding and thoughtful responses, it encourages us to open up even more, creating a virtuous cycle of trust, intimacy, and connection.

Encouraging Emotional Growth: Lastly, this practice of being vulnerable and responding thoughtfully encourages emotional growth in both partners. It teaches us to handle difficult conversations with grace, to understand the power of our words and actions, and to build a relationship that's rooted in empathy and understanding.

By intertwining vulnerability with the practice of responding instead of reacting, we're not just building a relationship; we're cultivating a sanctuary of trust, understanding, and deep connection. So, as we move forward, let's carry this toolkit with us—the courage to be vulnerable, the wisdom to respond thoughtfully, and the knowledge that in doing so, we are building something truly special with our partners.

Practicing vulnerability isn't always easy; it takes courage to show someone else your true self without fear or judgment from either side. But when done authentically, it can bring about some amazing benefits for both parties involved, including increased emotional intimacy, deeper understanding, greater trust, improved communication skills, better problem-solving abilities, stronger emotional intelligence, and even better physical intimacy. Yes, practicing vulnerability has been linked with higher levels of satisfaction in the bedroom as well!

Conscious Love

As we journey through personal growth and healing, there comes a point where we start to feel like we're thriving in our relationships. All the hard work and self-reflection has finally paid off, and we're able to show up as our authentic selves with our partners.

There will still be ups and downs and moments where we feel like we're back at square one. But, that's okay. What's important is that we're aware of where we are and continue to show up with love and compassion for ourselves and others. That's what truly embodies the healing work we've done. Being able to connect on both an emotional and physical level is essential for a healthy, loving, and fulfilling relationship.

When it comes to conscious love relationships, it's all about being present and aware of the dynamic between you and your partner. It's about being intentional in how you show up and communicate, being mindful of your emotions and boundaries, and always striving to create a space of understanding, trust, and mutual respect.

In a conscious love relationship, both partners are committed to doing the work necessary to maintain a healthy dynamic. This means having regular check-ins, being transparent with each other, and being willing to face challenges head-on together. It also means being open to growth and change, and recognizing that relationships are always evolving. In this type of relationship, as partners, you are encouraged to support one another in your growth, to learn how to love each other in new and deeper ways, and to bring your authentic and unapologetic selves to the table, without masks or pretense.

Now, pause for a moment to think about what that would feel like for you.

You may have a history of relational trauma or toxic relationships, and the possibility of leaving that behind might feel scary even if it's something you yearn for. These fears are why it's so important for us to heal and evolve; instead of remaining stuck in patterns of behavior that don't serve us, we can move to what we ultimately crave.

This is where conscious love comes in—a way of being with your partner that focuses on giving both of you the space to heal, evolve, practice self-regulation, and commit to listening, showing up with empathy, and honoring your shared meaning.

THE THREE PILLARS OF CONSCIOUS LOVE RELATIONSHIPS

At the core of any conscious love relationship are three key elements: respect, communication, and understanding.

- **Respect** means honoring each other's thoughts, feelings, and opinions without judgment or criticism.

- **Communication** is about being open and honest with your partner, sharing your thoughts, feelings, and needs without fear or shame.
- **Understanding** involves gaining insight into your partner's perspective—having empathy for their struggles and offering compassion when needed.

Bringing these three pillars to the forefront of a relationship can offer many benefits to both parties involved. When we cultivate an atmosphere of respect and understanding, it allows us to truly connect with ourselves and our partners in authentic, meaningful, and lasting ways. This kind of connection can be incredibly rewarding; it helps us build trust together while also deepening our self-awareness as individuals. Gaining an understanding of our own needs as well as those of our partner helps us make decisions that encourage stability and security—two essential core values we discussed in Part 1.

Let's explore what conscious love looks like in practice. Creating conscious love involves taking risks, opening up emotionally, letting go of control, and showing empathy toward each other at all times, no matter what life throws at us. By committing yourself fully to this type of loving connection, you will find yourself growing together with your partner rather than apart from them—creating shared meaning and experiences along the way. Here are some practices that allow conscious love to grow, as well as some quick tips on how to implement these practices into the fabric of your relationships:

Make Room for Each Other's Past and Growth

We all come with our own stories and, sometimes, baggage. In a rock-solid relationship, you give each other the space to deal with that and grow from it. Here's how:

Show Patience: Healing old wounds doesn't happen overnight. Give your partner time and space.

Support Their Growth: Encourage your partner to learn and grow, and be their cheerleader.

Keep the Communication Lines Open: Make sure you're both comfortable talking about the tough stuff.

Keep Your Cool and Really Listen

Knowing when to take a step back and cool off during an argument is key. And remember, listening is more important than being right. Quick tips:

Know When to Pause: Learn to recognize when a conversation is getting too heated, and take a break.

Practice Active Listening: Show that you're really paying attention, and make sure your partner feels heard.

Create a Judgment-Free Zone: Make your relationship a safe space for open communication.

Tune In to Your Partner's Needs

Relationships are a two-way street. It's not just about your needs; your partner has them, too. Make it a point to check in with your partner regularly about what they need. Try these:

Ask and Listen: Regularly ask your partner how they're doing and what they need from you.

Show You Care: Your actions often speak louder than words. Show your partner you're there for them.

Be Responsive: When your partner expresses a need, do your best to meet it.

Get Real About Feelings

Being honest about your feelings can make or break a relationship. It's not always easy, but it's worth it. How to do it:

Don't Hold Back: Share your true feelings, even if it seems scary.

Create a Safe Space for Sharing: Work on making your relationship a safe space for both of you to share freely.

Be There for Each Other: When your partner shares their feelings, show empathy and support.

Build Empathy and Shared Experiences

Understanding where your partner is coming from and sharing fun experiences can really strengthen your connection. Here's how to do this:

Show Empathy: Be there for your partner, especially when they're going through a tough time.

Make Time for Fun: Don't forget to laugh and have fun together. It's crucial for a healthy relationship.

Create Your Own Traditions: Having special rituals just for the two of you can bring you closer.

Choose Connection over Being Right

It's easy to get caught up in wanting to be right. But in the end, what's more important: being right, or being connected? Remember:

Focus on Understanding: Try to see things from your partner's perspective, even if you don't agree.

Learn to Apologize: Saying sorry when you're wrong goes a long way.

Keep Your Priorities Straight: Your relationship should be more important than winning an argument.

Turn Conflict into Growth

Arguments happen. It's how you deal with them that counts. Use disagreements as opportunities to understand each other better and strengthen your bond.

View Conflict as an Opportunity: Instead of as a battle, see arguments as a chance to grow together.
Stay Calm: Keep your cool, even when things get heated.
Work as a Team: Find solutions that work for both of you, not just one of you.

THE IMPORTANCE OF REPAIR

Learning how to repair after a conflict is an essential skill for deepening our connections with ourselves and others. When we experience conflict, it can be easy to feel disconnected, hurt, or frustrated. Repairing the relationship allows us to rebuild trust and restore our sense of safety and security.

Repairing the relationship with ourselves begins with cultivating self-compassion. This involves acknowledging our mistakes and treating ourselves with kindness and understanding. Through self-awareness, introspection, healthy boundaries, and higher standards, we can learn to recognize when someone isn't good for us. We can also learn to regulate our emotions and practice self-soothing when we feel dysregulated, which can help us communicate more effectively and navigate conflict in a healthy way.

When repairing relationships with others, it is important to approach conflict with empathy and validation. Empathy allows us to see the situation from the other person's perspective and understand their emotions and needs. Validation involves acknowledging the other person's feelings and experiences, even if we don't necessarily agree with them. When both parties feel heard and understood, they are more likely to experience safety and connection.

It's also important for both partners to meet each other where they are in terms of their emotional needs. This means being willing to compromise and make concessions where appropriate. It also means being open and honest about our needs, and being willing to listen to and support each other.

Through empathy, validation, and self-regulation, we can deepen our connections and create a sense of safety and security in our relationships. By meeting each other where we are at and practicing healthy communication, we can cultivate healthy relationships that are supportive, loving, and fulfilling, pushing us closer toward living as the best version of ourselves.

Creating a conscious, meaningful relationship is all about effort, understanding, and being there for each other when it really counts.

Conclusion

Navigating the New Upper Limit

L iving a more conscious life and practicing conscious love can be transformative. But it's hard to realize that we may have been settling for less than we deserve in our life and relationships. We need to navigate a new upper limit in our life and relationships, one that is based on higher standards, healthier boundaries, and shared core values.

Healing is a journey that involves facing and working through our emotional pain, trauma, and negative patterns of behavior. When we engage in this process of healing, we experience a rebirth of sorts, where we are able to shed our old ways of being and step into a new version of ourselves.

As we go through this rebirth, we deepen our emotional intelligence, emotional depth, self-awareness, and self-concept. Emotional intelligence is the ability to recognize and understand our emotions, as well as the emotions of others. When we heal, we become more attuned to our emotions and are better able to navigate them in a healthy way. We also deepen our emotional depth, which is the ability to experience and express a wide range of emotions. Through healing, we become more comfortable with our emotions and better at expressing them in a healthy way.

Self-awareness and self-concept are also deepened through

healing. As we work through our emotional pain and trauma, we become more aware of our thoughts, feelings, and behaviors. This increased self-awareness allows us to understand ourselves better and make more intentional choices in our lives. We also develop a more positive self-concept as we learn to love and accept ourselves for who we are, rather than feeling shame or self-doubt.

Healing also deepens our personal integrity, which is the alignment between our values, beliefs, and actions. As we work through our negative patterns of behavior and beliefs, we are able to align our values and actions more closely. This alignment helps us feel more authentic and true to ourselves.

Another important aspect of healing is our ability to create emotional safety within ourselves and others. Emotional safety is the feeling of being secure and comfortable in expressing our emotions and being vulnerable. When we heal, we become better able to create emotional safety within ourselves and in our relationships. We learn to be more empathetic, compassionate, and attuned to the emotions of others, which helps us create a safe and supportive environment.

To be intentional with ourselves and our relationships, it is important to continue to prioritize our healing and growth. This means being intentional about setting boundaries, prioritizing self-care, and communicating our needs and feelings in healthy ways. It also means being intentional about the relationships we cultivate, seeking out those who share our values and support our growth.

The rebirth that comes with healing deepens our emotional intelligence, emotional depth, self-awareness, self-concept, personal integrity, and ability to create emotional safety within ourselves and others. By being intentional with ourselves and our relationships, we can continue to prioritize our healing and growth, creating a more fulfilling and meaningful life.

Acknowledgments

I extend my heartfelt gratitude to the incredible people who made this book possible. To my clients and Inner Circle members, your unwavering support, encouragement, and belief in my work have been the driving force behind this endeavor. Thank you for speaking my name in rooms my feet hadn't entered yet.

Carol, your vision in recognizing the light within me and your desire to share it with the world have inspired me beyond measure. Your enthusiasm for my work made this happen.

Bryn, I am deeply thankful for your guidance throughout this writing journey. Your wisdom and expertise have been invaluable, guiding me with a steady hand and a push when I needed it.

Johanna, you've been the iron fist and lace love I needed throughout this process. Your unwavering belief in me and your unique blend of strength and compassion have been a source of inspiration.

To each and every one of you who have supported me on this path, thank you from the bottom of my heart. Your presence in my life has made a profound difference, and I am truly grateful.

With immense appreciation,
Ginger

About the Author

Ginger Dean is a psychotherapist and founder of Loving Me After We. Her specialty is helping women overcome heartbreak and increase self-love and confidence after a toxic relationship so they can become the best version of themselves.

www.lovingmeafterwe.com